The Akashic Record Player

Some Other Titles from Falcon Press

Antero Alli
   Angel Tech: A Modern Shaman's Guide to Reality Selection
   Angel Tech Talk (audio)
   The Eight-Circuit Brain
   8 Circuits of Consciousness (video)
   An Interview with Antero Alli (video)
   Paratheatre: A Ritual Technology for Self-Initiation (audio)
Christopher S. Hyatt, Ph.D. & Antero Alli
   A Modern Shaman's Guide to a Pregnant Universe
Christopher S. Hyatt, Ph.D.
   Undoing Yourself with Energized Meditation and Other Devices
   Radical Undoing: Complete Course for Undoing Yourself (videos & audios)
   Energized Hypnosis (book, videos & audios)
   To Lie Is Human: Not Getting Caught Is Divine
Christopher S. Hyatt, Ph.D. with contributions by
Wm. S. Burroughs, Timothy Leary, Robert Anton Wilson et al.
   Rebels & Devils: The Psychology of Liberation
S. Jason Black and Christopher S. Hyatt, Ph.D.
   Pacts With the Devil: A Chronicle of Sex, Blasphemy & Liberation
   Urban Voodoo: A Beginner's Guide to Afro-Caribbean Magic
Peter J. Carroll
   The Chaos Magick Audios
   PsyberMagick
Phil Hine
   Condensed Chaos: An Introduction to Chaos Magic
   Prime Chaos: Adventures in Chaos Magic
   The Pseudonomicon
Joseph Lisiewski, Ph.D.
   Ceremonial Magic and the Power of Evocation
   Kabbalistic Cycles and the Mastery of Life
   Kabbalistic Handbook for the Practicing Magician
Israel Regardie
   The Complete Golden Dawn System of Magic
   The Golden Dawn Audios
   The World of Enochian Magic (audio)
Steven Heller
   Monsters & Magical Sticks: There's No Such Thing As Hypnosis?

For up-to-the-minute information on prices and availability, please visit our website at http://originalfalcon.com

The Akashic Record Player

A Non-Stop Geomantic Conspiracy

by
Antero Alli

THE *Original* FALCON PRESS
TEMPE, ARIZONA, U.S.A.

Copyright © 1988 C.E. by Antero Alli

All rights reserved. No part of this book, in part or in whole, may be reproduced, transmitted, or utilized, in any form or by any means, electronic or mechanical, including photocopying, recording, or by any information storage and retrieval system, without permission in writing from the publisher, except for brief quotations in critical articles, books and reviews.

International Standard Book Number: 978-1-935150-61-9
ISBN: 978-1-61869-610-6 (mobi)
ISBN: 978-1-61869-611-3 (epub)
Library of Congress Control Number: 2015905762

First Edition 1989
Second Edition 2015
First eBook Edition 2015

Cover artwork by Shekinah Errington & Lynette R. Cook

The paper used in this publication meets the minimum requirements of the American National Standard for Permanence of Paper for Printed Library Materials Z39.48-1984

Address all inquiries to:
THE ORIGINAL FALCON PRESS
1753 East Broadway Road #101-277
Tempe, AZ 85282 U.S.A.
(or)
PO Box 3540
Silver Springs NV 89429 U.S.A.
website: http://www.originalfalcon.com
email: info@originalfalcon.com

ACKNOWLEDGEMENTS

Somehow, the following individuals were either indirectly &/or directly responsible for provoking me into writing and producing this book:

MICHELE & CAMILLE...*for inciting the miraculous amidst the MESS*
JOSE ARGUELLES...*for voicing the Earth through your Zen wave form*
KALLISTA...*for the steadiness of your gaze and changing my life forever*
CHRISTOPHER S. HYATT...*for the insights, the shocks and...the laughs!*
CHRISTI...*for the undeniable cocoon*

FRONT COVER ART
Shekinah Errington (jukebox)
Lynette R. Cook (starscape)

"HUNGRY ALIENS" PAINTING
Michaell Allen

ALL INSIDE CHAPTER HEADING ART (except where noted)
Roberta Jones-Wallace

WAVE-FORM SURFING
Christi Alli

REALITY SELECTION
Roxanne Dale

Thank You

For my three daughters

Kallista, Zoe, and Arizona

THE RECORD SELECTION

Acknowledgements 5
Introduction 11
Boulder, Colorado USA 15
Hungry Aliens 20
Reality Selection 26
Vintage Chaos 30
Future Memory 45
The Sphere of Sensation 59
The Goddess Guild 71
Vertical Stability 88
Tremble the Ground 106
Magnetic Arrangements 122
Wave-Form Surfing 134
The Killing Time 147
Additional Akashic Recordings 160
    Man/Woman/Planet: Earth Surrender Rites 161
    Campaign for the Earth by Jose Arguelles 165
    Interview with Jose Arguelles: When the Light Hits, the Dark Gets Tough 168
About the Author 177
Urban-Shaman Workbooks 178
Afterword 2015 186

INTRODUCTION

I don't know what this book is. It's not a novel or an autobiography nor is it a self-help, how-to manual. Maybe you can tell me what it is. As close as I can tell, it's a story about certain miraculous interactions. In fact, most people I tell this story to dismiss its notion altogether or change the subject. Maybe "most people" **aren't supposed** to understand this stuff and the few that do, should maybe hold meetings and talk about it and do rituals or, something. I guess it began when my friend, Jose Arguelles, showed me a photo of the legendary Face On Mars (see *Planetary Mysteries* by Richard Gossinger; North Atlantic Press) and offered certain notions of how it got there. Thereafter, certain events leading up to, including and following Harmonic Convergence also contributed to the miraculous. (See the Interview with Jose Arguelles later in this book.)

Sometimes, to keep my head above water, I sift the miraculous through a mythic, allegorical context. This does not mean that what you are about to read is "unreal" or that it did not happen. On the contrary, it is quite real and it happens all the time. Myth, in the tradition and spirit of the late great Joseph Campbell, is **the very language of life** and through its articulation, we can become *more alive.*

This myth is **geomantic,** or Earth-based, in that the primary player is the planet or, more precisely...**the planetary entity.** During this mythos, affairs between human players are sometimes secondary to their interactions with the planetary entity...whose interchange with interstellar entities (like Stars and Alien Space Beings), influence the course of human evolution.

True to their intention, **myths never really explain anything**. Yet, they truthfully convey a set of actions provocative enough to engage our emotions while transforming our vision. Human beings need myths like they need handles...to open doors...to catch a ride, or just to have something to hold onto. When did we start needing handles? Why do we have to hold onto our hats?

Myths are like dreams in that without them, we're as good as dead. However...dreams can be dangerous. Anybody living with one they are unable to manifest, articulate and/or share has, perhaps, already begun losing their handle. In the face of unknowns, I appreciate handles. They let me float in the abyss, knowing there is a grip to return to somewhere. Occasionally, I feel the only real handle there is, is my physical body. It's a relief to release that grip on occasion—to collapse, drop my big act and "die."

Much of this myth is historically true while other sections remain hysterically real. What you read into it is the narration of your own story. What you get out of it is my gift to you. The players' names have been changed to protect the innocent, save for Dr. Christopher S. Hyatt, who is neither innocent nor guilty, but a living, breathing, human being. Through his audacious compassion, he has helped me sort out which handles are actually attached to something useful and which ones are merely disconnected handgrips.

Since most of this story unfolded in the university mountain town and "new age mecca" of Boulder, Colorado...I've decided to preface it with certain statistical facts alongside my own idiosyncratic impressions of the place. I believe in the power of places. I tend to think that "being in one's place" is synonymous with good timing, and by coinciding with one's placement, a kind of synchronicity is released.

Every place has a unique energetic intention of its own. This is why certain kinds of activity tend to work better in certain places over others. For example: sites with a previous history (like theatres, churches, and town halls) tend to encourage the activities it takes to express its unique intention. Yet, 1 continually ask myself: **Why and how does a particular region or geographical locale get its intention in the first place?**

All places are united by being common expressions of the Earth. Why have human civilizations and their cultures localized in certain areas over others (besides the obvious commerce of ports)? From a geomantic perspective, cultures are geologically **formed entities** shaped by the topography and overall placement of their specific location. As Arguelles so adroitly puts it: *The Earth evolves us* (see *Earth Ascending*; Bear & Co.).

Gene pools develop culture out of intimate interactions with their immediate womb environment. Or, in Dr. Hyatt's words, **"Culture is NOTHING BUT the interactions between Genes and Geography"** (see *A Modern Shaman's Guide to a Pregnant Universe*; Falcon Press). This book was written in Boulder, Colorado...USA. Today, my purpose in Boulder feels completed, and tomorrow I move Northwest.

ANTERO ALLI
AUGUST 18, 1988

BOULDER, COLORADO USA

1

"If you don't like the weather, just wait five minutes."
Anonymous Boulder Weatherman

    The sunbaked auburn brick Boulder Post Office building is the secret epicenter of town. I know. Every morning, I make my daily routine drive there to get paid. Ever since I can remember, I've always derived simple pleasures from receiving mail...especially messages from people I've never met. Only now, there are cheques...enough of them to pay rent, gas the old Datsun and feed my bi-monthly sushi habit. Money's funny. It took twelve years of abject, food-stamp poverty to comprehend the arcane concept of **economic non-locality**. I never realized how much I took my environment for granted until I stopped relying on its economy to survive. Gradually, after many months of economic non-locality, nature's colors regained their hues...shifting sky-scapes came into view and the land splendorously opened up.
    The Earth is very prevalent here in Boulder, even unavoidable...with the magnificent Rockies in stark view, and the nearby flatirons slanting vertically into bright blue skies. The sun shines about 333 days of the year, contributing to a predominantly "solar" climate no matter how cold it gets in the winter. It's real dry...so dry that mid-winter frostbite warnings go into effect to remind people how it always **feels** warmer than it really is outside.
    Imagine now...one sleepy, global village nestled up against a mountain...where quaint, urban architecture replicates a Walt Disney movie set and people walk around entranced by the subtle dangers of becoming Disneyland versions of themselves. Imagine, too, a place where homeless street people look happy and **the artists don't know what to do.**
    Despite the hundred-plus registered religions sharing status with the emergent New Age Entrepreneurs, and the twenty-six year old average age of its citizens, Boulder is pretty much Anytown...USA. It's easy to overlook the discreet yet immense Buddhist community, the well-organized underground of

Rajneesh **sannyasins** and the 96% all-white population. Perhaps Boulder isn't that "ordinary" after all. On my more imaginative days, Boulder is a suburban Venus flytrap, seducing stray insects inside to explore its exotic intestinal tracts.

Closer to truth, I am more like a caterpillar locked inside a cracking cocoon, awakening to the first signs of future life. These signals are few and fleeting, with no certainty or promise of revealing itself beforehand. With wings restlessly rubbing against each other, one eye looks through the crack of my bulging cocoon and sees nothing...or rather, a darker shade of dusk. Fortunately, a blunt patience has grown out of the long wait...a calm burning from the inside. Without it, I think I'd have withered away inside the cold, quiet terror of one long, drawn-out dawn.

Why do certain people migrate to certain geographical locations at certain times in their lives? What draws someone to one place over another? Is it a job opening...or nearby family...or are there educational opportunities? Or...are these superfluous, yet distinctly human excuses masking a greater engagement between our particular organism and a specific planetary region? What does the Earth want from us, anyway?!

I think Boulder is one of those places that holds people to itself for specific purposes until *it's* ready to let them go. This is how the sub-title of this book came to pass. I don't think Boulder's the only city or place that has a mind of its own, and I don't believe I'm the only one who has had a difficult time leaving. This *non-stop geomantic conspiracy* appears in more dramatic ways with some people than others, too. I've heard Indians say that nature spirits are very strong in this area. Is that why every third person I meet has a quote or opinion from their local, neighborhood shaman? Or was that just another barking dogma nipping at my heels?

Boulder has this propensity for behaving like a giant spiritual petri dish...sprouting tangles of hybrid cosmologies, mushrooming philosophies and extraterrestrial fungi. This tends to produce a kind of time-warp factor in the social environment. People seem to meet each other exclusively by arrangement with

Boulder, Colorado, U.S.A.

The No Coincidences Dept. Some serendipitous meetings look like damned good stage magic. Others unfold naturally inside what appears to be clockwork synchronicity, which is so thick at times you can slurp it with a spoon.

The peculiar geomancy, or "earth spirit," here encourages certain activities while almost forbidding others. Micro-cultures of experimental social forms tend to thrive. A group process forms around almost every occasion imaginable, from feminist men's groups to collective bike riding to VCR preppy parties. What doesn't seem to do well here is Dangerous Art...you know, the kind that wakes people up. When people wake up here, they tend to migrate or go back to sleep.

Boulder's abnormally low crime rate and artistic poverty provide inhabitants with an unusually high level of personal asylum and safety. Sheltered from the uncertainties of big city life, Boulder offers a place to retire from worldly concerns while rewiring for the future. Many people arrive to get married, die &/or give birth to themselves before migrating. Then, like any other place, there are the "lifers" who so accurately personify the spirit and look of the newly, emergent society.

Living here has elicited, deep within my little zen heart...an irreversible, poetic anarchy. Don't get me wrong...nothing as artless as common, political anarchy could ever stir my blood. I don't even like the best political street theatre (San Francisco Mime Troupe). It seems to me that a well-placed **propaganda bomb of new information** is plenty to sabotage anybody's outdated dogmas. It can perform more justice to a fragmented society than any form of physical violence or satirical ridicule, whatsoever. Besides, I'm totally unconcerned with the banalities of "changing the world." As far as I'm concerned,

it's far too late for anything but magick

as the future is clearly

UP FOR GRABS.

2

Boulder is a germinating city gestating its future history as a cutting-edge proponent of the post-information, Consciousness Age. The blue-collar jobs of the future belong to Space Industry burn-outs and Computer Hackers. Until then, futant human seedlings face the emerging terror of the current era…

INFORMATION WARFARE!!!

Right now, there are so many conflicting sources of information regarding the nature of reality that anybody who isn't thinking for themselves (by now) is probably losing their minds. Historically, wars have been fought over territory. Here in the Information Age, the human mind **is the new turf** and battle strategies are being designed this very moment to destroy, maim, claim, and/or govern as many personal noggins as possible. So, my friends, hold onto your trick tophats…a human mind is a terrible thing to waste.

The new martial info-disciplines will train **INFO-Warriors** to tolerate greater doses of uncertainty so as to minimize the immobilizing tendencies of settling down into Pat, Easy Answers. INFO-Assassins of the Mass Media, New Age, Old Age, and Middle Aged can now be seen everywhere spoonfeeding the soft, muddled-class minds with the **Anti-Improvisational Sedatives of ANSWERS.** Answers ought to carry the Surgeon General's WARNING:

ANSWERS may be hazardous to your Uncertainty.
Danger! ANSWERS carry High Overdose Potential.
Remember: ANSWERS are the Thrill That Kills.

JUST SAY NO (thank you) to…
ANSWERS

And, while you're at it…enjoy the show.

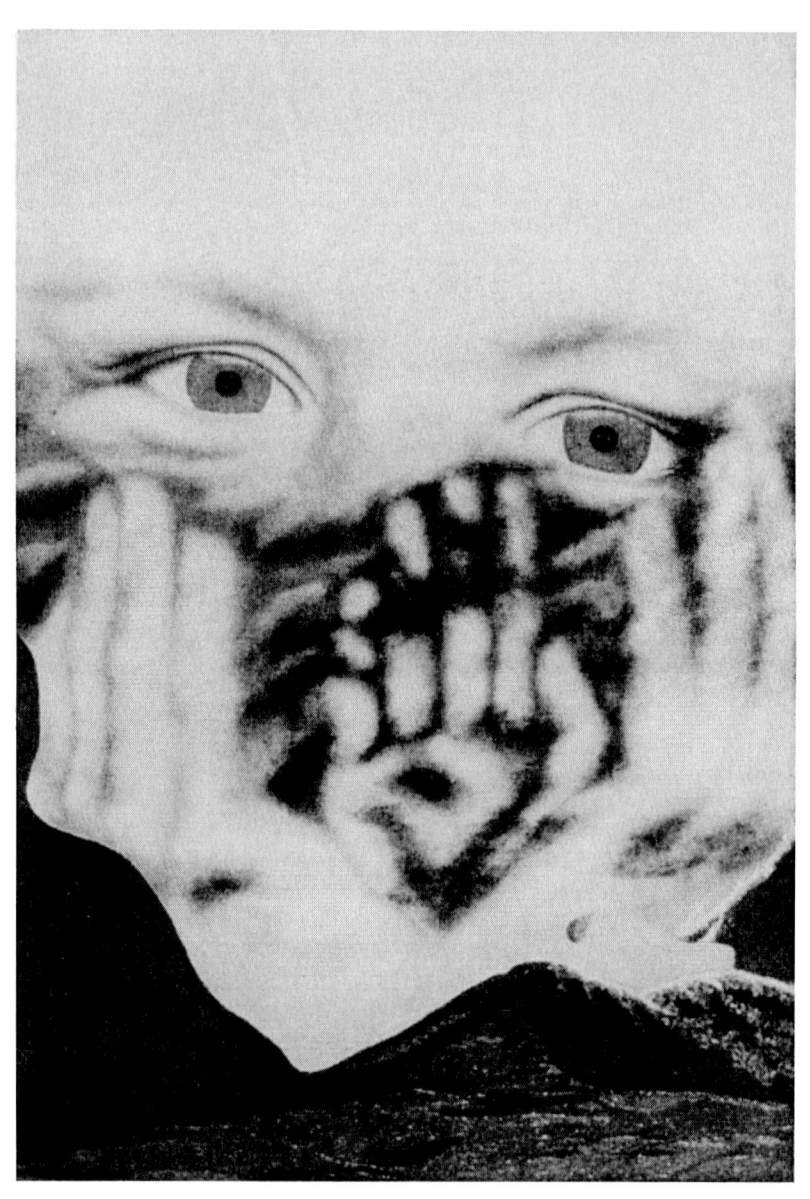

HUNGRY ALIENS

1

Aeons ago, in the lost era of our Ancient Heritage, ALIEN SPACE BEINGS arrived and impregnated our planet with the seeds of their future harvest. They were Aliens because they are not originally from this planet. They were Space as they were extremely intelligent. They were Beings as long as they held conscious intention, which they did. As interdimensional shape-shifters, Alien Space Beings travelled between the third, fourth and fifth dimensions...changing form to adapt to the diverse survival conditions of their daily lives. They elected a council of **spirit farmers** to be responsible for feeding and nurturing their interstellar family. Spirit farming entailed the locating of a biologically responsive planet and the planting of **spirit seed** inside suitable neuro-muscular organisms to eventually produce a non-stop crop of spiritual food. Since Alien Space Beings were essentially immaterial spiritual entities, their survival depended on certain high-frequency, vibratory substances.

Before their arrival, PLANET MIRTH was a wild, overgrown oceanic garden teeming with multitudinous species of flora, insectoids, reptiles and primate mammalia. It was with the latter that Alien Space Beings grafted their spirit seed into for synthesizing a hybrid now called "human being." Over the millennia, Planet Mirth has since been renamed "Earth" to identify itself as an interstellar agricultural center. Its purpose was the production of enough spiritual food to assure the survival and evolution of the Alien Space Beings. Like any other crop, this one required certain culturing processes before it could be harvested.

With their advanced tuning systems, Alien Space Beings amplified the communications network connecting our planetary entity, its closest star and the galactic core for optimum informational exchange. The activation of this trinary intergalactic circuit released enough essential nutrients for catalyzing the growth of human **cultures** around the planet's surface. Through numerous stages of **human** evolution, these cultures matured into civilizations by constant interaction with the planetary entity. A few, like Atlantis, Lemuria and Egypt, outlasted the rest, but eventually collapsed to fulfill the Earth's interstellar, agricultural function. The ripening of the alien spirit crop always paralleled the individual human shift from a **vertically-stable spiritual** orientation to a more **horizontally-active material** identification.

As soon as vertical internal reliance was replaced by complete horizontal dependency, a human being *lost* **its** *soul.* This soul, along with countless others, was assimilated into the alien harvest. The greatest harvest always followed the crest and downfall of a civilization; the larger the civilization, the greater the yield. Every twenty-four thousand years or so, Alien Space Beings celebrated the sweetest, most abundant harvest of them all. In astrological terms, this occurred at the end of every Piscean Age whereby human evolution revolved almost entirely around elaborate forms of religion-worship…producing vast horizontal feeding frenzies called "Holy Wars." This time was referred to, by Alien Space Beings, as **The Great Collapse** and it was always a time of tremendous human sacrifice and massive suffering. It was during The Great Collapses that the compassionate intelligence of the planetary limbic system also underwent its most profound development.

As the Earth's largest civilizations were inadvertently yet routinely preparing for the next Great Collapse, the planetary entity busied Herself with new expressions of Her boundless love. Over the millennia, She grew increasingly aware of a handful of human beings that chose to remain true to their vertical, spiritual orientations rather than lose their souls in another horizontal, spiritual catastrophe. Through the rise and fall of Her world cultures, She assessed that perhaps **eleven percent** of Her human crop remained vertically loyal to Her. This **geomantic, microculture** selected to derive its stability, strength, wisdom and morality from **direct resonant relationship with the Earth.** These humans, She felt, were not destined to become food for Alien Space Beings but deserved to be born as baby gods from the womb of Her omni-directional consciousness.

As part of Her evolutionary imperatives, the planetary entity was preparing to relay a new signal to the Alien Space Beings regarding Her service as an interstellar garden. She was also ready to communicate pure gratitude to the Alien Space Beings for allowing the deepening love of Her children. To propel this transmission it was necessary to locate and train certain human midwives to birth Her baby gods. Each midwife had two parts… one negatively charged and the other, positive…one human woman and one human man. These humans were selected from the geomantic micro-culture and…for the high-frequency, electro-magnetic charge oscillating between them. In other words, only certain men and certain women were able to contain and direct the Earth's energy, appropriately.

Most often, these select men and women started out with only the faintest notion of what was happening and why they really met. They would, however, inevitably realize their experience was set apart from the rest of the human population by their reluctance to **Fall In Love, Get Married, Have Babies and Buy Furniture.** This didn't mean they didn't try to do these things. It's just that these cultural definitions of coupling failed to contain the intensities required to birth the baby gods within them.

2

The physical fate of planet Earth gathered momentum by spinning through deep space, following the trajectory of its orbit around its closest star. The planetary entity expressed its spiritual **destiny** by what and how it chose to develop on the way there. As part of Her destiny, She arranged for meetings between certain men and women by awakening in them an awareness of their shared fate. She also subjected each man and woman separately, yet simultaneously, to certain **shocks**…to open and prepare them for the **Intensive Care Unit,** where these three operations took place:

I
EARTH SURRENDER RITES
Activities arousing an **ongoing awareness of and reliance on the planetary entity** *as a source of vertical, internal stability.*

II
POLARIZATIONS
The **articulation and integration of internal polarity** *towards establishing and activating humans as bio-electromagnetic batteries, or power sources.*

III
CEREMONY
The **flexibility** *by which human bio-electromagnetic batteries interact amongst each other while engaging the geo-electromagnetic battery and energy field of the Earth. The activation of the Man/Woman/Planet trinary interactive circuit.*

The planetary entity prepared Her midwives by instructing them to perform these three operations **on purpose.** Each man and woman learned to recognize Her instruction by the repeat appearance of **multiple coincidence** surrounding each lesson. As the midwives executed each operation, the frequency of multiple coincidence *accelerated.* By the stabilizing influence of Earth Surrender Rites, midwives were able to regain placement and...navigate through the turbulence of quickened coincidence, or **synchronicity.** Once the commotion settled down and synchronicity became the **Standard Time Zone,** the planet went into labor.

The Planet Earth Is In Labor

AND

We Are the Mid-Wives

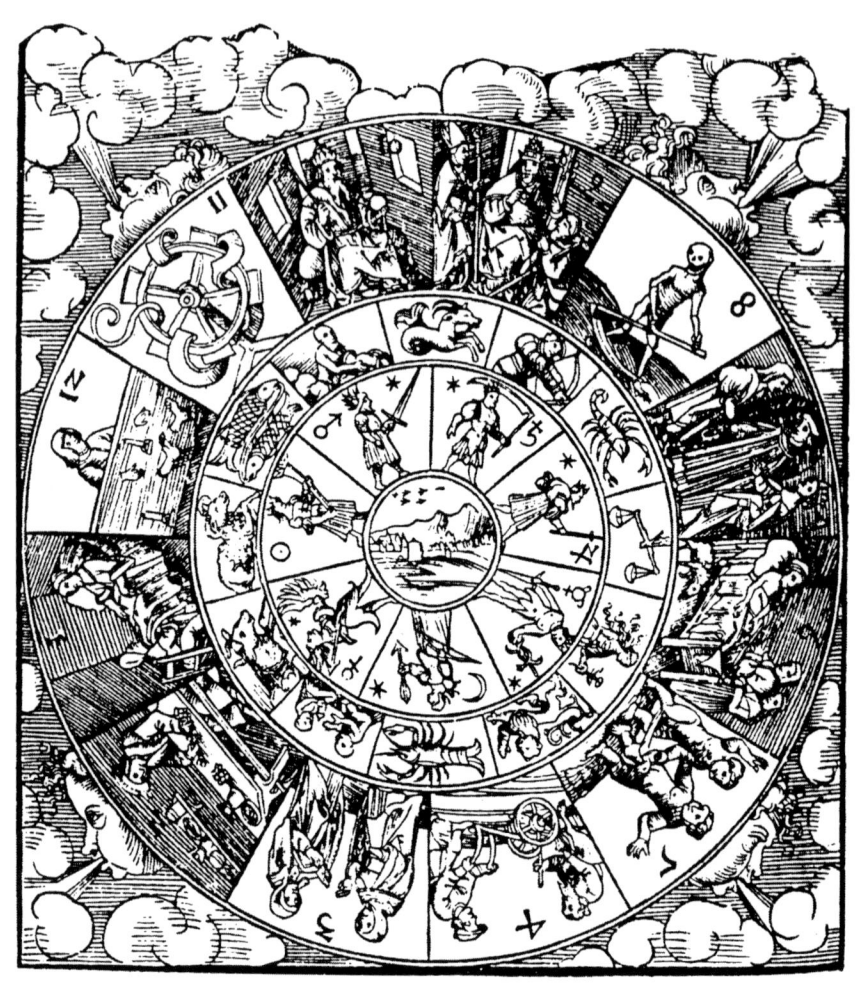

REALITY SELECTION

1

"Chance favors the prepared mind..."

The planetary entity and its human inhabitants are, for the most part, not on speaking terms any more. This is partially due to the accumulation of an excessive, static "grey noise" generated by the unavoidable side-effects of a mechanistic Industrial Age. Its pervasive electro-chemical pollution has all but buffered humans from the direct resonant relationship normally affording their sense of placement as planetary midwives. This story conveys certain attempts at establishing communications between the planetary entity and its human inhabitants during **The Great Collapse of 1987–92**...a highly critical stage of their mutual future history.

2

The communication style of the planetary entity is broadband, multiple frequency transmission. Its *modus operandi* is not unlike a high-powered, broadcast radio-satellite simultaneously transmitting multiple messages. Now, as a rule, most human minds can usually only permit one thought or concept at a time. The occasional irregularity emerges with those minds willing and able to permit enough **uncertainty** to beget an awareness of **multiplicity**. This presupposes a recognition of and participation in a **multidimensional reality**...wherein *all dimensions are equally valid aspects of a greater changing whole.* Preference for one level over another, at any given time &/or space, is a matter of **personal style**. If there was a name for this multi-purpose brain function it might be :

reality selection...
*a prerequisite for hearing
the multi-vocal planetary entity.*

As humans *endure* the multi-faceted awareness of simultaneously converging information sources, they learn to **dial and fine tune** those frequencies appropriate to the concerns of the time and place they are in. With persistence, the development of a **reality selection circuit** (in the Central Neural System) encourages High-Velocity Interaction with other humans **by virtue of tolerance.** (As humans distinguish and qualify various levels within their own being, they tend to tolerate internal contraries thus, vicariously, allow for differences in others.)

> Tolerance of differences
> **minimizes inertia**
> *by maximizing flow.*

By allowing for the unpredictability of simultaneous truths, certain humans start growing more receptive to signals beyond the realm of their own minds. It is here in the Concept-Free Zones where humans can unwrap their high-frequency antennae from self-preoccupation and direct it towards each other...and down to the planetary entity...on up to the stars and...beyond. Perhaps, humans may be free to restore their service to the planetary entity and eventually...establish membership in an intergalactic federation of vertically-stable Alien Space Beings.

3

In addition to its own indigenous voices and frequency shifts, the Earth is a local resonant conductor for non-local, extraterrestrial transmissions. Alien Space Beings and other interstellar entities broadcast messages via DNA, **the native language of the Planetary Entity.** Consequently, these signals traverse throughout all living forms on Earth. Those humans, awakening to the ongoing dialogue between their individual Central Neural Systems **(CNS)** arid their originating DNA coils, are now subject to **intergalactic influences.** Eighty-nine percent of the human population is unable to tolerate the impact of such direct spiritual transmission, so...the socio-moral inertias of religions and/or philosophical grids have been superimposed to **slow things down**.

This same CNS/DNA interaction is known by many names as each culture assigns their own conceptual bias to this universal truth...i.e.,

Jesus & the Christ... Gautama & the Buddha...

but more specifically...
a Human Being & the Planetary Entity...

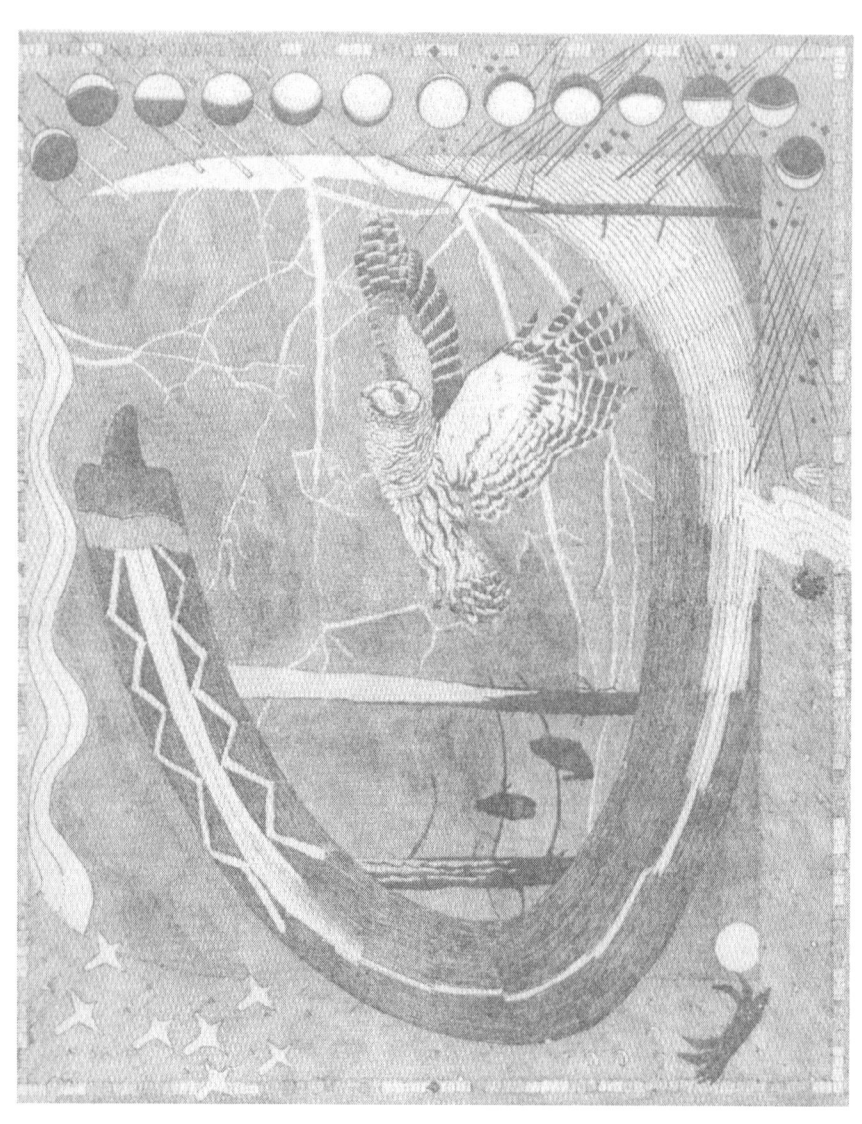

VINTAGE CHAOS

1

"A chao (pronounced 'cow') is a single unit of chaos...therefore, chaoboys and chaogirls wear designer genes of future myths..."
excerpted from THE 23 ERISIAN MYSTERIES

Time: *The Great Collapse (approx. 1987–92)*
Place: *A record skips inside the AKASHIC RECORD PLAYER*

In the House of the Rising Sun...k! Rising Sun...k! Rising Sun...k! Rising Sun...k! Rising Sun...k! Rising...

"Get that, will you?!"

Sun...k! Rising Sun...k! Rising...

Thank you. Good information's expensive...in fact, it's pure hydrogen, burns like hell, illuminates heaven and consumes the best of minds and, by the way...we open no-mind before its time. Siriusly though, it's only natural that your Brilliant Ones sought cool, dark places for refuge... where they de-crystallized while learning the Hedonic Arts of Falling Apart. No entity at this time could've predicted the devastating side-effects of that much extended trancework, not even Seth. See Jane. See Jane run...see Jane run too much energy. She could have neutralized the psycho-active states of her chosen profession instead of short-circuiting like that. Periodic rapture and profound bliss are still used as trance-dispersion devices in fourth-dimensional Atlantis. Unfortunately, most of your early Psychoids were primitivists...natural talents...and thus, somatic idiots incapable of turning themselves on if they were left alone inside a magnetically-charged, Dakini Ecstacy Chamber with a fully-accredited Tantric Zen Mistress.

Listen...entity to entity...who am we? **In Lake'ch...I am another yourself** *except...I am multi-vocal...I speak in many tongues, languages and frequencies. Yet, I am still an entity like yourself...only larger. I have incarnated* **as this planet. I am now the Earth.** *I am also pregnant. I'm recovering from a rather torrid romance with the* *interstellar father of my unborn children, who has left me to give birth alone. There are baby gods incubating in the womb of my omni-directional consciousness. They are seeking out human cocoons to birth through.*

I am arranging for the midwives to meet and perform the necessary ceremony to save my children from the hungry aliens. If you don't believe me, you can always change the channel…no matter where you go, here I am.

2

Time: *One Friday twilight in Early Summer, 1987*
Place: *An overgrown field overlooking suburbia, Boulder COLORADO*

Camouflaged by the lush, tree-lined gully across the street from the middle class bungalows, members of the Temple of Erisian Deities (TED) ate pizza while awaiting their prime time attack signals. Everyone ate pizza before breaking-and-entry. This assured the consistent signature of someone defecating on whatever they collectively designated as the altar of each and every home they burglarized. According to them, houses were latent temples activated only by strategically engineered outside shocks. The collective mission of the TED was, of course, to provide this necessary incentive for restoring genuine holy terror in the hearts of the households they eventually converted.

The TED observed how each house revolved around a slightly different point of worship…a charged psionic area unveiling precisely what the inhabitants lived for. It was the TED's unique karmic service to clarify this altar. Sometimes, it was the vanity desktop in the master bedroom…other times, where the television sat before they lifted it. On other occasions, it was either on the stove or inside an oven or in the refrigerator. It mattered little to them whether or not that home's inhabitants, upon returning, understood their intentions. The TED knew their impact and unanimously agreed to a common destiny of service to the hodge-podge divinity of ERIS: Goddess of Chaos, Holy Discord and Foreign Policy.

The dogma of TED stemmed from their conviction of imminent, nuclear catastrophe...inciting within their wild discordian hearts a white-hot compassion towards anyone who had still not heard "the news." Their self-appointed mission was almost always directed towards *domestica de suburbia*. They believed that the Middle Class, Judeo-Christian doctrine of Armageddon cloaked a dangerous, irreversible death wish. According to the TED, biblical doomsday prophecies carried a self-fulfilling, religiously-enforced outcome reminiscent of outright nuclear warfare.

The TED's task force dedicated itself to the disillusionment of the Middle Class before the blistering, sub-atomic flash of hydrogen atoms did it first. The TED were also convinced that a group called The Future Furniture Buyers of America set into motion a sinister conspiracy of social control by successfully over-domesticating the American people. They also believed the FFBA to be directly linked to the Fundamentalist Christian Republicans and, indirectly, to the declining post-hippie, New Age movement.

THE 23 ERISIAN MYSTERIES is the holy scripture forming the backbone of the TED. Its first axiom, "Today's star is tomorrow's black hole," was engraved in every member's immediate neuro-memory. It held the TED together as an all-star, no-star congregation with a rotating altar and the polarized leadership of a high priest and priestess. Raphael, the high priest, was a young man in his late twenties severely disturbed by visions he spread like a fever amongst the rest. Savitri, the priestess, was carried by the presence of an avenging angel...her dark fiery eyes searing through the pale, glacial beauty of her fine-boned face.

Scoping the virgin temple through his binoculars, Raphael chewed on the end of his pizza crust while nodding his freshly, shaved head in steady approval. Savitri glanced sideways at him. "It's that time, isn't it?"

He continued chewing the crust while nodding. "Yup, yup, yup…"

She turned to the rest of the young men. "Showtime…" Murmurs of soft chuckles came and went. Silently, they all wiped their hands on the moist towels included in their preparatory ceremonies for temple construction.

3

Time: *The Great Collapse*
Place: *The MYTHIC ARCHIVES, Planetary Psi-Matrix Memory Net*

Here's an Indian Bedtime Story. The current Hell Cycles began when the White Minds crossed the Great Waters and anchored on the Land of the Red-Hearted Ones. There they met, broke and defeated the Red Hearts. Blood was spilled and heads, they rolled. Thirteen hundred moons later, the Souls of the dead Red Hearted warriors reincarnated as the newborn of the White Minds. These new Red-Hearted Souls were recognized by the Red Hearted Ones of that time by the way they dressed and wore their hair to look like the Red-Hearted. The first wave brought the "hippies" who marked the beginning of the end for the White Minded. One-hundred and thirty moons later, the "mohawk punk fashions" signaled a new wave of Red warriors and two-hundred and sixty moons afterwards…crystal channeling, pop shamanism and Mayan nostalgia. This is how the Red Hearts initiated the Great Collapse and finally defeated the White Minds. The Reds were defeated because of their weak hearts and the Whites, their weak minds. For now we know what happens when a people's strength grows too strong…yang turns to yin, hurly burly hits Broadway and everybody is hereafter proclaimed a Pope.

Is Nothing Really Sacred? Of course it is, my cherry blossom...of course, it was...

4

Time: *Later on that same Friday night, Early Summer 1987*
Place: *A suburban house in Boulder, Colorado, USA*

> "You were reaching out, expecting to connect with a real person, weren't you? Well, you can be sure we understand how you must feel after hearing this mechanical, recorded message. We're sorry we can't be here for you now but if you leave your message after the tone, we'll return your call as soon as possible. Take as long as you like and no matter what, expect a miracle..."
> **(Bleeeeeeeep!)**

"Hello...Angel? This is Gabrielle...jesus...I wish you were there. Something awful happened. Call us as soon as you get in, OK? Bye..." Putting the phone down, Gabrielle cautiously walks throughout the house which used to be her home but was now transformed into a hideous labyrinth...every room, another chamber of chaos. Adam, her fiancé, paces in the backyard looking for clues...anything to help him understand why it happened. Gabrielle doesn't need to know why; it was clear to her what happened. They had been broken into, violated and raped of their right to a secure home.

With a puzzle erupting up through his face, Adam peers upward to the starry Colorado sky. "They knew what they were doing. But why...why? Why now and...why us? They stole my computer and god knows what else and, Gabrielle... Gabrielle..." He hears her scream and suddenly turns, running back into the house calling her name. "Gabrielle... Gabrie-l-l-l... Gabe!!!!?"

Her soprano scream sings its way out of their bedroom, bouncing off the walls through the hall where he now stands transfixed. An infinity later, Adam bolts for the bedroom. There, from the doorway, he sees her crying, covering her mouth, eyes frozen with horror at the fluffed up pillows near the head of their custom-designed, queen-size waterbed. A choked laugh coughs itself up from his diaphragm, "Holy shhh…" He looks at her and she looks at him. They were both too afraid to do what they really wanted to do more than anything else…to laugh…to laugh so loud they couldn't hear themselves cry…to laugh so hard their adult faces could crack open and fall off…to laugh so long they could fly into each other's hearts again. Neither laughed. Adam spoke through the tension. "I guess I'll go call the cops…"

She winced in embarrassment and shrugged. "Guess I'll clean up the mess."

5

Time: *8:23 AM, the next morning*
Place: *ANGEL DAYCARE CENTER, Boulder COLORADO*

The sing-song chiming of happy toddlers rings throughout ANGEL DAYCARE when Gabrielle arrives for work. Hanging her purse on the hook by the door, she heads out towards the backyard. There Angela, the supple young Mother Goddess, holds…feeds…and watches her menagerie of assorted children. Gabrielle steps out onto the back patio just as the telephone rings. Angela's radiance overlooks Gabrielle's forlorn state, while cheerfully waving to her. "Oh, hello Gabrielle…could you get that?" Gabrielle mechanically turns around, walking back into the house towards the phone. The answering machine goes on before she gets there.

Angela sings from the backyard. "Who is it?"

Gabrielle appears on the sunny backyard patio again. "I don't know…the machine got it. Sorry I'm late. Did you get my message last night?"

Angela takes a second look at her, surprised by what she now sees. "You look a mess. What happened? No, I didn't. What happened?"

Gabrielle's eyes shift around the backyard as she half-explains herself. "We were broken into last night. It was awful…they took the stereo, the TV, Adam's computer, my jewelry. I feel so violated…totally humiliated."

Angela puts one child down while lifting another inside the nearby playpen. "I suppose you already called the police?"

Distracted, Gabrielle's words stumble out. "Yeah…they said our…thing…was just another…in a whole series of similar things. They're all done by the same gang, they're pretty sure… because of the way all the places were left after being hit. You're right…I am a mess. I think I need some time to myself and…"

Angela sighs and looks at her watch. "No problem…I think I can get a replacement if you're not up to it…if not, I'll cope."

A dark, guilt-ridden glance shoots out her eyes. "Are you sure? I mean, it's not very professional of me but I'm…just absolutely wrecked."

Angela looks at her then, looks down to the ground. "No, it's not professional and yes, it is OK. And yeah, you do look wrecked. Call me when you feel better. Call me anyways, OK?"' She turns around and picks up a hungry, wailing toddler. "Oh, pooooorrr babbbbyyyy…"

Before Gabrielle could respond, a three-year old red-haired girl suddenly appears from behind and surprises her. "Say thank you, lady…"

Gabrielle jumps and an involuntary "thank you" pops out of her mouth.

6

Time: *The Great Collapse*
Place: *DREAMTIME SWITCHBOARD, Planetary Crystal Gridwork*

*We are now being dreamed by those human forms who are feeding the Dreamtime with their sleep. Humans can experience two major dream paths in their **nightmares and revelations**. Nightmares feed the spirit world by the fear they instill, vacating the human form and inviting various disembodied spirits to eat the mind. Fear is ghostfood and death to the mind. No daring is fatal and waking up is an act of unnatural courage.* **Children have nightmares in order to wake up.** *By waking up inside their dreams, humans inspire revelation and inform the dreambody of its true intention. The dreambody can then awaken to itself by…**intentional spin.***

  The dreambody is your totality as human entities and every whole, no matter how small or large, spins and generates its own measure of density, or gravity. The hearts of all heavenly bodies are created from an ultra-gravitational force called love. Your willingness to surrender to its influence ushers you through nightmare and into revelation. An unswerving self-commitment is paramount to this initiation which intersects the dreambody and the earthbody. As the dreambody, you can choose to be born inside your human forms as they sleep. This way, you will not be recognized too soon and can permeate the biological machine from within without alerting its primitive mind to the miracle of your presence. Remember, in the blessed realm of manifestation…gravity is not just another good idea…it's the law.

7

Time: *7:27 AM, August 15, 1987*
Place: *The bedroom of Gabrielle and Adam's House, Boulder CO*

The man and woman sleep curled around each other, sending spirals into the Earth below until she moves…opens her eyes, then squints them closed again. The spirals expand, breaking and blending into the Earth…her eyes slowly re-opening…absorbing the sunlight gliding through the crack between the curtains. The two human forms shift their weight…tossing and turning, blindly searching for their next mutual shape to resettle in.

Open-eyed, the woman gazes into the rays of sunlight, absorbing more particles into her awakening mechanism. She turns her head to the man and considers touching him, decides against it. "Adam? Are you awake?" The man grunts disapproval while pulling the sheet over his head. "I guess not…"

She quietly rises out of bed, pulling her nightgown over her head while stumbling through the hallway into the bathroom. Here she sits naked, pondering her reactions to the dream she is awakening from. "Wonder if it meant anything… Maybe it's enough that it just happened…like maybe, it doesn't have to mean anything. Maybe **I'm** enough just because I'm happening. I dream, therefore I am?" She laughs while the phone rings across the house in the kitchen. "Take it away Mr. Message Machine…"

The machine suddenly clicks, releasing its live message into the kitchen air. "Hi, Gabby! Sorry for calling you so early but something's happened. There's this new psychic in town and I just thought you'd like to know about him. He's not one of those wimpy, Neo-Christian lightworker channels. He's got an extraordinary energy all his own and…"

Gabrielle runs into the kitchen and grabs the receiver. "Hi Suzanne, what's up? What's all this about a psychic?"

"I just got a reading from him last night and it triggered all these outrageous dreams and…like…I was initiated inside this awesome temple into a kind of death/rebirth ceremony to bring the murdered son of a goddess back to life again. Totally strange, Gabby. I don't think it was just a dream, Gabby and I really need to talk to you about it."

Gabrielle shakes her thick mane of dark, curly hair. "I should've been there, right? Listen, I've got something to tell you, too...yeah, why don't we meet around twelve-thirty at the Saturn Cafe, OK? OK...bye..." Gabrielle slowly pivots around and walks back through the hallway towards the bedroom, turning back only to look at the bed where Adam lay motionless, asleep.

8

Time: *12:32 PM, August 15, 1987*
Place: *The SATURN CAFE, Boulder CO USA*

There was always a certain stillness pervading the Saturn Cafe. No matter how many people were there, they all seemed to be suspended in time...mindlessly reading, drinking espresso or watching the door for incoming action. A kind of atmospheric density anchored the place. Like re-entering the Earth's stratosphere from deep space, one could anticipate an initial shock of discomfort until adjustments were made to accommodate gravity's everloving commitment.

Gabrielle's shift usually came as a sudden, shrinking self-consciousness which she learned to mask by entering the cafe with her sunglasses on. She removed her French-design eye-protection only after arriving at her designated landing target... usually a table in one of the far southwestern corners. Suzanne's adjustment occurs in just the opposite manner. The internal pressure of the Saturn Cafe elicits her posing tendencies, puffing her ego out like a multi-colored parachute to soften the re-entry impact. Once at the table, however, both gradually join the anonymous repose highlighting the transient members of their local group mind at the Saturn Cafe...

9

Time: *The Great Collapse*
Place: *Planetary Optic Nerve Center—PARADISE CENTRAL—*

For those of you viewing EARTHWATCH on your new, revised **Select-A-Visions,** *soon you will recognize that familiar face as your own. Throughout the duration of their Great Collapse, it has been designated mandatory procedure* **for all human visionaries** *to be* **seen** *as often as they see. We, at PARADISE CENTRAL, encourage all psychics to detect and integrate local community status priorities for securing the necessary recognition for re-charging your central nervous systems. These emotional coordinates eventually fulfill the interdependence of spiritual and material wealth...requiring of your human life a greater degree of* **being rich and happy.** *As you burn into your human forms, their matter converts into your energy as mega-photons of impersonal charisma released into your immediate social vicinity. You are stars in formation. This stellar information has been brought to you direct from your non-local* **Select-A-Vision** *sponsors at PARADISE CENTRAL. Your local program may now resume.*

10

Time: *12:24 PM August 15, 1987*
Place: *The SATURN CAFÉ*

SUZANNE
So, why do you think it's over between you and Adam?

GABRIELLE
You could keep your voice down. I didn't actually say it was Over. It's just that he fits all my pictures and that makes me nervous. It feels a little unreal. It kinda caught me off guard.

SUZANNE
Are you sure you really want to get married?

GABRIELLE
I don't know…maybe…I think so…but maybe not to Adam. I just don't feel that certain about him.

SUZANNE
How can anybody feel certain about anyone or anything these days?

GABRIELLE
I don't know…I'll know as soon as I meet him…my body will know…

SUZANNE
You mean, if your heart doesn't leap out of it first.

GABRIELLE
Ha! Right. No, I'll know…instinctively, I'll just know.

SUZANNE
How? How can you know?

GABRIELLE
I'll get real still in his presence…a kind of burning calm.

SUZANNE
Hubba, hubba, cha cha cha…just what do you mean, Gabby?

GABRIELLE
Excitement isn't everything, Suze. Don't you believe in spiritual love?

SUZANNE
Only in the movies. At that, only those made forty or fifty years ago…

GABRIELLE
Well, I do…a kind of love that hasn't happened before or maybe used to happen aeons ago before everything got so twisted and knotted up. Besides, I think the world needs a new kind of love, don't you?

SUZANNE
Goddess knows we've tried everything else…

GABRIELLE
And it's got to be a kind of love that doesn't…"try."

SUZANNE
It's true, it's true…I hate trying. Trying is so…dismal.

GABRIELLE
Dismal…abysmal…oh so, dreary…

SUZANNE
Why do I always feel like I'm in a movie around you?

GABRIELLE
Simply dismal, my dreary…you wouldn't want to know…

SUZANNE
Try me.

GABRIELLE
You love watching people's private moments. You've got camera-shutter eyes, Suzy…the kind that takes everything in. Sometimes, I feel like I'm in a movie around you. I mean, I've never told you this before, but there are times I perform for you…in subtle ways

and, in not so subtle ways. You bring me out of my shell and…I like that. Yet…there's always something about you that's not entirely with me…something really detached and aloof…even clinical. I mean, I can't say I totally trust you, yet I can always rely on your perception. Oh yeah, I love how psychic you are.

FUTURE MEMORY

1

*"And the women's stratified lunar eyes: Eyes of dreams which seem to absorb our own, eyes before which we ourselves appear to be **fantome**."*
ANTONIN ARTAUD, on Balinese dancers

Time: *Sunrise, August 16, 1987*
Place: *A desa (village) in West Bali, Indonesia*

Just before the Balinese sunrise, pre-Atlantean birdcalls awaken mesozoic memories in the hollow wails of abandoned dogs possessed by Hungry Ghosts stalking the volcanic grounds of the village. These canine gargoyles continue to serve, as they have for aeons, the disincarnate discontents who own and live through them, and so, they are protected and nobody bothers them. They roam free but are never satisfied, no matter how much they eat. Some die hungry from debauch. Others contend with their fate by non-stop yelping seizures…snapping frenzies. Most, however, keep moving…from village to village, with an occasional pilgrimage to the foothill jungles of the mountain to either breed or, die.

The sun rises. Its cool, golden radiance glides across the eastern slopes, illuminating the huts perched high on slanted stilts. The humans sleep. Everyone else flies, sings, leaps, and crawls into the early morning weave of dawn. Out of the flurry, a human lightbody appears…returning to the central neural system of its particular human form…igniting…waking it up. Its biological male apparatus moves, mechanistic and slow. First, an arm, then…an eyelid. As more synapses fire, its head rises and suddenly jerks to the left…away from the sun, collapsing back into the pillow…releasing the dreambody out for more fourth-dimensional work. The dreambody drifts away from its biological anchor, disappearing…shifting back into the dreamtime, the early morning glory in its wake.

The Earth was unusually quiet. Her serenity deepened as She was slowly fed and then, made love to by Her favorite interstellar entity. There were no earthquakes today nor any need for volcanic eruption or atmospheric pain. Inside this brilliant, gentle sunrise...Mother Earth ecstatically absorbed the superluminal signals from a distant galactic core, pumped by Her lover into Her fiery, crystal heart. She was taking in every quantum wave of hot galactic love. Aeons of patience poured into this luminous moment that, to human measure, lasted a full day...when 144,000 humans greeted the dawn in complete surrender to the Earth and, through Her grace, walked away with new fires burning in their hearts.

Up the path, leading to one of the stilted huts, walks a young Balinese woman carrying a small basket of flowers. Climbing the rope ladder, she ducks slightly through the entrance where an American man lies sleeping on the mat by her feet. Bending over, she places the fragrant flowers by his face while gently provoking him with her outstretched foot. "Michael... Michael...wake up now...it's harmony converging time..."

The dreambody returns the instant the flower's essence mingles with his olfactory nerves, opening his eyes with a small, enraptured smile. "Dewi...I had the most extraordinary dream..."

She impatiently nudges him. "Michael, the sun has already risen. We will miss the harmony converging if we do not go now."

Michael laughs softly. "That's *harmonic convergence* angel, and we're not missing anything. It's all happening right here and now in this very hut. My dream said it all. I've got enough information now to get us both out of here. Listen...all we have to do is ground it out...feed the planet with the excess psychic energy we've been holding onto between us and then, vamoose...leave town..."

Visibly disturbed, Dewi protests. "What do you mean, Michael? Not again! Why do we have to leave? This is my home. My family is here. You talk nonsense again. No more."

Michael rolls his large blue eyes up into his head. "Dewi, don't even try to understand. If you were to awaken to your true identity now, it would blow your ship right out of the water and probably everyone else's around you...including me. I mean, I could tell you who you are but it probably wouldn't make any difference."

Amused, Dewi prods him. "Tell me, Michael. Tell me who am I?

He laughs. "OK...I am now resting at the feet of the pre-Atlantean lineage of the twenty-third crown princess of the Sirius Star system. There! Does that make any sense to you? Probably not, right? Right. No problem. However, if we don't get you out of here pronto, you'll never find out...not in this lifetime anyway. Your wonderful culture is so damn gorgeously oppressive that if it weren't for me, you would've never even heard about Harmonic Convergence, Crystals, Channeling, Sirius, and all the other amazing things I've taught you since we met. Don't you see? You have to leave this place to realize who you are. Don't you see that, angel?"

She masks her impatience by a smile. "Michael...what did you dream?"

He sits up, stretching his jogging-built body. "The dream? Picture an Atlantean temple...with this woman, who might've been you, preparing this ceremony to feed the planet. You see, somehow I had to direct our energies down to the Earth's core somehow. The temple was collapsing and the Earth needed to be fed before everything fell apart. That's why I've got to send our energies down before the shit hits the..."

She interrupts him. "Michael, let's go to the mountain now. The sun is already big in the sky..."

"Good idea, Dewi...good idea..."

2

Time: *1:23 PM, August 15, 1987*
Place: *The SATURN CAFE, Boulder COLORADO USA*

Several young men from the Temple of Erisian Deities arrive, ushering Raphael into the now busy Saturn Cafe. Like some repellant force-field, their entry style bounces back the attention instantly sent to them by the post-cappuccino, sedentary nervosa of those seated around them. The TED appear, socially, as fashionable anarchists...bright-eyed, young, angry men in black with black-dye, chaotic hair. This public image kept most people at a distance, creating an antisocial ambiguity the TED took solace in. This is also why everyone looking at them now began averting their gaze for fear of finding out what they really didn't want to know. That is, everybody except Suzanne who could not keep her eyes off Raphael as he lounged down around a table with the others across the room.

GABRIELLE
Have you decided what you're doing for the Convergence?

SUZANNE
I'm not deciding...(laughing) I'm waiting for my DNA-pak to arrive. I figure I'll know at the last moment, and then I'll just follow instructions.

GABRIELLE
That's pretty much my plan, too. So, you still haven't told me anything about this psychic. I mean, is he cute or what?! He is a he, right?

SUZANNE
Definitely a he. And definitely not cute unless you like "strange." I mean, you know me. I stopped going to psychics ever since the channeling epidemic brought on this awful New Age Miscarriage.

GABRIELLE
New Age Miscarriage?! That's rich, Suze. It's true though...it looks like sell-out time. I feel real sad about it, too...kinda like when the whole hippie thing died and everybody stopped believing in all the great new ideas that made life back then so much fun. I mean, I remember worshipping my older brother when he'd come home from college, from Berkeley, and tell me all about the protests, drugs and communes and stuff.

SUZANNE
It was American history, to be sure. I think something like the Sixties will happen again though real soon...like maybe the

Nineties. I think it'll have to be more organized this time. Or else, we might as well just forget it.

GABRIELLE
Yeah...so, listen...why did you see this particular guy...what's his name?

SUZANNE
It's...it's...that's funny, I don't remember. It'll come to me. He's written some books, you know...

GABRIELLE
He's an author?

SUZANNE
Yeah...and apparently he lives around here part-time.

GABRIELLE
That's a good way to live around here...part-time. Interesting...he's pretty discreet...I mean, I haven't heard of anybody new and I'm usually the first to know around here about this stuff.

SUZANNE
He doesn't advertise. I found out about him kinda by accident through a friend of a friend. It was more like synchronicity...you know Boulder. Without going into all the details, let me just say it was truly amazing. He sat in a chair across from me and started seeing through me. He told me secrets about myself...gave me dates, names, numbers...real specific shit! Then, he asked me to watch my dreams that night and those dreams were gorgeous...great, hot dreams...

GABRIELLE
What do you mean...great, hot dreams?!

SUZANNE
Pure information. It was like reading the most brilliant science-fiction while having multiple orgasms in a tanning salon. Great hot dreams...

GABRIELLE
What kind of information?

SUZANNE
Relationship stuff. Stuff about men and women feeding the planet with all that excess energy built up between them, instead of having it turn into stupid stuff...like fighting and shit. Too bad I forgot most of it.

GABRIELLE
Yeah, too bad...sounds like I could use some of that information now. I woke up after some pretty wild dreams myself...

SUZANNE
Gabrielle...you must get a reading from him.

GABRIELLE
That's probably a good idea. Do you have his number on you?

SUZANNE
You don't need it. Relax...he's sitting right behind you.

Gabrielle casually glances over to the table where the TED sit, sipping exotic coffees. Raphael fixes his line of sight just to the right of her gaze, somehow causing her to turn abruptly to face Suzanne again.
    Gabrielle gasps. "God, he's intense. You didn't tell me he was...so..."
    Suzanne feigns nonchalance knowing she is now watched by Raphael. "Young? I forgot...it seemed totally irrelevant. He does look a lot younger here than yesterday. I guess his face changes when he does that stuff. Whatever he pulled down into himself was pretty ancient, though. Well...are you going to do it or not? You know, I can introduce you..."

    Gabrielle fidgets. "No, not just yet...let me think it over. You do have his number?"
    "Yeah, yeah. Not on me. Call me later and I'll get it for you. Are you sure you don't really want to set it up now? I mean, he's right there and..."

Gabrielle looks around again determined to sustain eye contact with him. Her eyes search for his before realizing they're gone...all of them are gone. Mildly aghast, she wonders out loud. "Whose movie is this, anyways?"

3

Time: *The Great Collapse*
Place: *PLANETARY NEOCORTEX, Future Memory Sector*

Your Higher Self is nothing less than that part of your totality which has already realized its destiny and awaits the rest of you to catch up. Of course, it wouldn't hurt to appeal to this "future self" as it does, indeed, find this most appealing. You can do so by flexing your future memory. What silver sliver of your mysterious being is beckoning you to become more of what you already are, what you have always been and are to realize in your becoming? You see, who you are in the present is but a fragment of an outwardly expanding ripple originating from the center of who you have already become **in the future.** *You have already happened, my little leaf. The colorful autumn of your sleep has arrived. Do you know who you are? Do you know that you are? We know that you are. Do you know who I am? Do you know* **that** *I am? Do you? We do, don't you?*

4

Time: *Mid-day, August 16, 1987*
Place: *The Jungles of West Bali, Indonesia*

Michael and Dewi are lying naked...entwined together, high above the surrounding jungles on a large volcanic rock. Their bodies undulate in pulsating unison, their minds oblivious to anything beyond the rapture expanding between them. Suddenly, the sounds of shuffling bushes and men's voices interrupt their reverie. Dewi panics, digging her fingernails into his bronzed back. "Michael... Michael...someone's coming..."

His movements quicken and deepen. His breath shortens as the two continue their lovemaking despite the attention they are now receiving from the swiftly approaching Balinese Police. "Michael...stop...we must stop now!"

Michael moans, ejaculating as he sees the police climbing the rock towards them. With a soft cry, he rolls his eyes up into his head. "Whose movie is this?!"

5

Time: *The night of August 16, 1987*
Place: *Police Dept., Downtown Denpasar in Central Bali, Indonesia*

Three young Balinese policemen speak their native tongue amongst themselves, while keeping close watch over an obviously distraught American male citizen. One of the policemen barks, "Sir!"

Michael responds immediately. "Yes?"

Handing him his passport, he stares at Michael. "Your visa has expired."

Michael takes it, acting surprised. "I didn't know that, I'm sorry."

He scrutinizes Michael. "Why are you here?"

"As a tourist. I'm on vacation."

One of the two policemen behind the spokesman asks Michael a question in Balinese. Michael shrugs. "Do you understand or speak Balinese?"

"No, I don't."

The policeman looks away then, directly at Michael. 'Why were you with this girl?"

"Uh...we like each other. She's my girlfriend."

The police laugh. "Her father says you were trying to kidnap her." Taking a deep breath, Michael shakes his head. "Her father is an important man here. If he is right, then I'm afraid you must go to prison."

Michael collects his thoughts. "Dewi and I met at a festival and we just became friends. We are just friends...we are very good friends."

The police speak rapidly with each other, glancing to watch his reactions. "Do you have any plans to bring her out of this country?"

Michael speaks firmly. "No, I don't."

"Can you prove this?"

"Yes. I'll leave right away... I'll even leave without her."

The police all nod, in broken unison, exhaling and relieved. "Yes you will. This is best."

A question swells up from Michael's heart. "Can I, at least, say good-bye to her before I go?"

The police all look at each other in utter disbelief. "I'm sorry, sir but I'm afraid that is quite impossible."

6

Time: *10:32 AM, August 17, 1987*
Place: *Gabrielle and Adam's House in Boulder, Colorado, USA*

Gabrielle looks out the window of her disheveled living room to the crystal-clear, warm summer day beyond. Her mind drifts in and out of the room, contemplating her conversation with Suzanne. Behind her, Adam shuffles around the house picking up after himself. He sees her standing there staring out the window. Entranced by her silhouette, he stops.

"What are you doing today?"

Ever so slightly, her body contracts. "I don't know...how about you?"

"If I can find my other shoe I'll be going out to do some shopping for us. It's been awhile, you know. I mean...ever since we got broken into, it seems things haven't really gotten back to normal... know what I mean?"

"Normal…what's normal?" Her blank tone makes Adam laugh. They both laugh. She turns to him. "OK…normal means the relative standard by which one measures consensus reality, right? Normal is changing, Adam. I don't know exactly how or why but I'm starting to feel like our vandals actually did us, or at least me, a favor."

His eyes meet hers. "Like shaking rotten apples out of the tree?"

She turns away again. "Rotten apples don't grow on trees, Adam…"

He walks over to her, touching her waist with his fingertips. "How have we been lately? We keep missing each other. We're never around…it's like we have different shifts or something."

"It feels good to hear you voice the obvious. I am feeling kind of shaky…I mean, our distance is no secret and we haven't really talked about anything yet. I know how you hate processing stuff with me so…I've just kept it to myself, more or less. Other than that, I couldn't feel better, really." She turns to him, hands outstretched inviting him into her arms, where he gently collapses. "We're friends. This much I know. I love you. I know that, too. It's just that something has been dislodged in me and its taking its sweet time floating up to the surface. I feel like my cocoon has cracked and it's dark outside and I'm not a butterfly yet. I'm sorry if this is creating anxiety for you. It's just the way things are right now…"

He hugs her tight. "You don't have to explain yourself… I mean, I don't understand what's happening either but I'm OK with it, most of the time. I love you, too…" They both squeeze each other tighter and then she suddenly lets go, looking into his eyes.

Adam breaks their silence. "Thank you, Gabrielle…thank you for just being you."

"It's a job. Look, I don't mean to break up a good thing, but could you get some Tabasco sauce for me when you're out in the world of shoppers?" He laughs. "By the way, you'll find your mysterious missing shoe under the bed where you last left it."

Adam lets her go and heads down the hallway into their bedroom, sighing to himself, "Where would I be without you?" Gabrielle enters the kitchen, picks up the phone and calls Raphael.

7

"Hello...if you're hearing me now, I'm gone or I'm monitoring this call. Worry not...my ultra-magnetic recording mechanism has been diligently trained to absorb your signals and rearrange them into readable messages. If you'd like, you can start your transmission after the high-pitched squeal that will be your cue to make a statement about yourself...and remember, don't assume I'm not nearby hanging on your every word." (squeeeeelch!)

"Great message. I don't even know your name but my friend Suzanne had a reading with you recently and I'm calling to set up an appointment. You can reach me at 444-(click)..."
 "Hello...stay put, I'm monitoring calls today. There. Yes, we've met..."
 "Not formally..."
 "About as formal as a shared hallucination at the Saturn Cafe..."
 "Well, yes, I suppose we saw each other there...I called to..."
 "...set up an appointment for a reading. I know. I heard your message. Why do you want a reading?"
 "Uh...I guess I need some perspective on some changes I'm going through."
 "Can I discourage you?"
 "Why?"
 "Let me put it this way. Can you be discouraged from wanting a reading from me?"
 "What do you mean? Why should I be discouraged?"
 "No, no, no...skip it, OK?"

"Well, maybe I shouldn't..."

"Yes, you can be discouraged and so maybe it's best we... don't."

"Wait a minute... I feel manipulated! [pausing, taking a deep breath] OK, yes, I want a reading and no, I'm not discouraged. How about this week?"

"Since you're not that easily discouraged, I'll read you. I'll be out of town until the 6th of September, though."

"How about September 7th, then. Do you have an opening at 8 pm?"

"How about seven instead?"

"Fine. How much is it?"

"Sixty dollars...cash, if you don't mind...and, you'll need to bring a 90-minute cassette if you want me to record it."

"7 pm on September 7th, bring a tape... OK...anything else? Anything I can do to prepare?"

"Just come as you are and pay as you go..."

"Oh, by the way, what's your name?"

"Raphael...but you can call me Raphael. Don't call me Ralph, ever."

"Hi Raphael, I'm Gabrielle. And where do I go to meet you?"

"Archangel Gabriel can go to the Boulderama Hotel, room number 230."

"Boulderama...room 230...OK..."

"Until then, Gabrielle...blessings."

"Blessings, Raphael." Both hang up their respective receivers at exactly the same time. Gabrielle enters Adam's office, turns on and boots up his computer and, starts writing up a storm. Raphael coughs abruptly and then, calls Savitri.

8

"Please excuse my answering machine's terrible manners but it only knows how to squeel like a pig when it's ready to be fed your message. And it's feeding time right now..." Squeeeeel!

"Lucy? This is Ricky. Lucy, you got some explaining to do! Babba looooo, honey. I'm leaving town to play the big Coconut Grove. It's real important, honey and I'm going to haveta miss our big anniversary party with Fred and Ethel, but I'll make it up to you honey, I promise, OK Lucy? What am I really sayin', honey? Don't do nothin' 'til I come back, OK? We gotta cool out on those religious practices until I get back. Tell the boys in the band, they'll understand...tell 'em Ricky's gonna talk to God, OK Lucy?! Until when, *mi amore...adios, muchacha.*"

Raphael slams down the receiver, walks over to the Buddhist calendar tacked onto the inside of his bedroom door and marks the date September 7th with a red star. "Whaddya know...full moon in crisis..."

THE SPHERE OF SENSATION

1

"Everything living on the Earth...people, animals, plants...is food for the moon. All manifestations of organic life on Earth are controlled by the moon. The mechanical part of our life depends upon the moon, is subject to the moon. If we develop in ourselves consciousness and will, and subject our mechanical manifestations to them, we shall escape from the power of the moon."
GEORGES I. GURDJIEFF, Dance Master & Sufi

Time: *Sunset, August 17, 1987*
Place: *Three Orchids Tavern in Sedona, Arizona USA*

The twisted, towering redrock mountains encircling Sedona contain a wide array of human foliage, silently sheltering its people like gargoyles guarding the threshold of some forbidden underground treasure. Here, people who are done with the world come to hide and/or die. Entertainment industry burn-outs, once-famous people and paranoid millionaires all number among the power elite. Some come to be transported by Sedona's alleged high-energy vortices into extra-terrestrial dimensions. Others arrive and end up settling down for the rest of their lives, as many more show up to just pass through.

Then, there are those few who prefer its vast, majestic beauty as a backdrop for the occasional business meeting. One such encounter was now taking place between a young author and his publisher inside a cool, dark tavern over expensive cognac and potential literary contracts. The publisher, a portly, muscular man in his mid-forties, lit the cognac-filled glass chalice with a match, enjoying its flaming bouquet before offering it to his author. Raphael took the glass to his lips, letting the warm velvet liquid slide down into his palate where it swam in circles. The publisher, who bore more than a cursory resemblance to a young Orson Welles, sat back...obviously enjoying every passing moment of their unfolding ritual.

"That's over a hundred dollars a bottle, by the way. Years back, when I was rolling in dough, we rented a Rolls, had a chauffer drive us all around France just to test the world's finest cognac wherever we went. Four, five hundred dollars a bottle some of it. [He burps out loud, then farts.] Pig! Who's a pig?!"

The young man laughs. "I've been meaning to ask you about that. How come every time you burp or fart...which seems often enough to me...how come you always accuse yourself of being a pig and then, immediately refute the accusation?"

"To break trance. It's a dismantling device I'm working with. Besides, if there's one thing Mr. Perfect should always remember it's that **we're all pigs.** Don't you ever forget that. Too many authors, especially as they grow more well-known, forget this simple barnyard truth and you better not be one of them. You're a pig. We're all pigs. Little piggies in a very big trough."

The young man was dumfounded. Instantly, he **knew** what his older friend was talking about yet could not fathom the implications he intuitively **felt** were there.

"Ralph...you ought to find your own personal devices to break your own trance. Writers, perhaps more than anyone else, are seduced by their work into a kind of **word trance.** Some of them are crafty enough to control it. Now, you're already smart enough to know the difference between the map and the territory but you're still hypnotized by the limitations of your own language. Word trance is our greatest downfall and, our greatest achievement. You see, it's really the old power of naming and the art of casting spells that determines our so-called reality tunnels..."

"What do you mean...the limitations of my own language?"

"New Age Cosmic Foo Foo! You're still a foo foo. You're from the foo foo camp, you see, and you're either seeking a cure or spreading the disease." Christopher burps loudly. "Pig! Who's a pig?!"

The embarrassed author laughs and inhales another sip of the cognac. Looking out the window at the blazing ochre Sedona sunset the author struggles with what has just been exposed in him. "You're right, Chris. You're absolutely right. I am hypnotized."

"A little less now but yeah, you are. It's not bad you know. It sells books for us. The Foo Foo market is cresting now and you're definitely a part of it whether you like it or not. You're not only a part of it, you're an expert...a fucking foo foo authority. You see, the downfall of the foo foos is that they're just like sheep, either getting fat for fleecing or for slaughter."

"Fleecing or slaughter, huh? What do you mean by *foo foo* anyways?"

Hyatt leans back in his chair, pondering his approach. "Well, the official word from Dr. Christopher S. Hyatt can be found by reading his controversial book, *Undoing Yourself with Energized Meditation and Other Devices*. But since you're my friend, I won't refer you to the scrolls. The foo foo mentality is spineless, existing pretty much from the heart on up in the so-called 'higher centers,' if you will...at the cost of losing touch with the so-called 'lower' or vitalistic chakras. As far as I can see, there's only one alternative left to open up those foo foo sacrums...only one everlasting, absolute perma-cure..."

Raphael winces. "What's that?"

Hyatt laughs out loud. "Are you ready? Brace yourself, Ralphy. **Crystal suppositories!**" Both men simultaneously keel over in laughing spasms. "And the real clincher is that they'll probably buy them and do it if they read it in a book or if someone tells them to!" Their laughter dances throughout the adjoining restaurant. "It's a new age commodity...the crystal suppository business!" The laughter crescendos and gradually unwinds after one prolonged, withering fart by Dr. Hyatt. "Pig! Who's a pig?!" He takes a cigar from his jacket pocket, bites off the end and lights it, puffing wildly. "Nothing like French cognac and a good, Cuban cigar..."

They raise their glasses in a silent toast and, drink it down. "You see, the New Age trance has occurred, in part, by a total misrepresentation of analogy. For example, Fritof Capra was unjustly deified for the *Tao of Physics*, which is based almost entirely on analogy, yet strongly suggests a whole lot more. Now you have to understand my bias as a hardcore empiricist. My background is, as you know, Reichian psychotherapy and previous to that…the hard sciences of brain research. Monkey brains."

Pausing to finish the last of his cognac, he savors the vapors filling his brain. "In the back, hind region of a male monkey's brain there's what's called an occipital lobe that regulates their sense of sight. Experiments have shown a direct correlation between visual stimulus and sexual arousal in male monkeys. Delete the occipital lobe and the male monkey loses interest in sex. Now, do human males depend on visual stimulus to maintain a state of sexual arousal? Based on my experiments with monkeys, **I tend to think so** but I'm not absolutely sure as I haven't witnessed this experiment with human males."

The bartender appears. Hyatt's brutishly eloquent gesture for a refill sends him temporarily away. "Now, when this lobe was removed in female monkeys, there was no visible lack of sexual arousal so we came to the conclusion that female monkeys do not require visual stimulus to be turned on sexually, but can rely on their sense of touch, smell, taste and so on. Now, if you ask me if this is true with human females, I would say…**I tend to think so**. But, I'm not willing to draw a total analogy as of yet, unlike the foo foos who constantly draw analogies everywhere in order to produce the comfy illusion of their so-called reality."

Raphael contemplates his words while scanning his mind for the appropriate metaphor. "Like marshmallow soup, right?"

"Like marshmallow stew. And it never satisfies, ever. That's why they remain trapped in their non-stop, horizontal feeding frenzy amongst themselves…chanting ALL IS ONE, ALL IS FOO FOO…not realizing how they're doing the exact same thing as our friends…the fundamentalist christians and the rest of the goddam muddled class…"

Raphael laughs. "Muddled class. That's great…"

The bartender returns with a fresh chalice of cognac, nodding his appreciation. "Yup yup! The muddled class are all instant candidates for the Future Furniture Buyers of America Reward… More furniture!!!" He burps. "Pig! Who's a pig?! Anyway, this pathetic lack of critical thinking reduces the foo foos to...foo foo...meaningless blobs of faceless energy...bland and homogenized...**like Cold, Boiled Jesus...CBJ...** Cold, boiled jesus...you know...the twice boiled, washed out, spiceless meat, potatoes and gravy the muddled class feeds their young all the time? Which reminds me. You haven't fertilized any eggs, have you Ralph?"

He looks up at Chris, quizzically. "Eggs? Oh, right. No, no eggs..."

Hyatt looks out over Raphael's shoulder to the reception area by the door. "Yummm, bacon!" Two well-dressed women appear through the tavern's front door, looking around the restaurant. "Yummm! There's a couple of hatcheries." Raphael turns around just as the women turn their backs and walk away towards the other end of the restaurant. "Sperm banks, all of them! Red, hot incubators. You know, a woman changes drastically after having a child. She is simply not the same person. That's why you should think thrice about fertilizing eggs if you really love and, especially, **like** the woman."

Raphael tilts his head slightly to the left. "How do they change?"

"Completely. I've been married thrice over and divorced shortly after having a child with the first two. I just couldn't live with her afterwards. I crashed and burned twice to figure that out. Those hormones don't stop until well after breast-feeding and as long as they're manufacturing those chemicals, they're almost entirely security-oriented creatures of the deepest habit imaginable." He takes a long, languid sip from his glass chalice. "DNA is a powerful drug so—it's not their fault, really. They can't help but be more demanding and needy with babies pulling on them all the time. They are clearly victimized by DNA at this point... robots for procreation locked into the security and territorial circuits with virtually no chance of escape. They almost stop becoming people with minds of their own..."

The bartender walks over. "Another round, sirs?" Both men nod in unanimous approval and then, Hyatt burps.

"Pig! Who's a pig?! So, women have it pretty tough. Their rights are naturally violated after childbirth, not only at home but in the medical community by the rapidly expanding **afterbirth industry.**"

"What afterbirth industry?"

Hyatt looks away in casual disbelief. "Yeah, didn't you know?"

He sighs, wearily. "I don't know if I even want to know."

"Yeah...the medical staff takes their juicy, protein-saturated placenta away from them and converts it into numerous products for medicinal purposes...cosmetics and drugs. It's proven almost totally effective for severe burns, for example. Yup yup. Afterbirth is a multi-million dollar enterprise."

Raphael sits in a bewildered trance. "I didn't know..." Hyatt looks at him for a moment, as if waiting for some kind of sign. "So, shall we get down to business?"

"Thought you'd never ask. As you know, both your books are doing fairly well...for starters, that is. We'll know a lot more after their second bulge, next year. Until then, I'd like to you to write another...only this time, together with me. There's a crucial post-new age concept I've been playing with lately."

Raphael's eyebrows slowly stretch up towards his hairline.

"What is it?"

"**The Cyber-Shaman.** *Cyber* comes from the Greek, meaning 'steersman or pilot' and shamans deal in spirits. Shamanism is hot now and will probably remain that way for a few years, at least. The cyber-shaman navigates the turbulence of the spiritual, or **neural,** world. I'm looking to set up a rebellious counter-movement to your so-called New Age, and I think this cyber-shaman idea is a good start. There's something dynamic about it. It's disciplined, technical, precise...qualities severely lacking in the foo foos. I think you're the one to write the book with me since you're one of their emerging mouthpieces or...nipples, if you will." He laughs long and loud.

Raphael sips his cognac. "Cyber-Shaman. Compelling synthesis...kind of like what I do anyways?"

"You got it...but don't forget, I named it. I want you to distill the essential technology from both your previous books and pack it into a much shorter version. I'll do the same and we'll co-produce it. Kind of like a handbook type of thing. If we do it right, we can go to market, have some fun and make a little money along the way. Who knows, we might even end up in the future history books?"

Raphael downs the rest of his cognac and gasps. "OK, I'll do it. When's the deadline?"

"We need to go to print by April, the latest. Is six months enough time?"

Raphael's studied deliberation catches Hyatt's attention. "I'll write it before my next tour."

"That's the spirit." Hyatt pulls out his wallet and starts writing out a check, glancing over at him. "Authors like you are far too few…you're not sitting around on your big flabby writer's cheeks waiting for some publisher to bend down and kiss them. We hate that *prima donna* shit and I'm eliminating writers right now just because they're out of control with it. Here's an advance to hold you over, dyke." He tears it out of the checkbook, handing it to him. "Let me know if you want anymore later. I might be good for a few more C-notes. Then again, I might not so don't hold me to it and don't forget you're a pig in a very big trough groveling about with a lot of other piggies." He burps. "Pig! Who's a pig?"

Raphael instantly responds and laughs. "I'm a pig."

"Yup yup. How's your temple construction homework coming along? You do have an ongoing group, right, and an ongoing place where you meet?"

He takes a long, silent deep breath. "Yes and no. Our official ecclesiastical title is The Temple of Erisian Deities. We've been experimenting with portable temples and rotating altars until we land a more stable place to work out of…"

Hyatt slams his pudgy fist down on the counter. "You need a stable temple, man. Fuck this portable stuff, it's far too advanced for you right now. Trust me on this." Hyatt leans back in his chair, his rugged features half hidden by the shadow behind him. His satyr-like face momentarily frozen pensive, he pulls another cigar from his breast pocket and lights it. "So…I suppose you got together with your foo foo hatcheries on your Harmonic Convergence and placed Mr. Happy on the altar?" He chuckles to himself.

Laughing uncomfortably, Raphael gradually looks away and out the window into the starry night. Hyatt smiles widely in wild anticipation. "Wel-l-l-l?! I'm waiting…"

"Christopher, seriously…or as seriously as you wish to be…what are your thoughts on the recent Harmonic Convergence event?"

"Seriously? My personal thoughts on the Homogenized Disturbance are, for the most part, unfit for print. However, I did enjoy what Bob had to say about it."

The young author's ego squirmed in his chair. "So…uh, what'd Bob say?"

Hyatt's laughter booms across the bar. "The yuppie rapture…the Harmonic Convergence was the goddam YUPPIE RAPTURE!"

He abruptly stops laughing to burp. "Pig! Who's a pig?!"

2

Time: *Later that night*
Place: *At the base of Bell Rock…Sedona, Arizona*

A circle of thirteen people sit at the foot of the natural stone altar chanting…low-pitched, guttural monotones. Against the black, starry sky, a silver crescent moon cuts its way over the horizon. The group's tone grows increasingly gruff and deep with the moon's ascent. Two members of the group see the moon and sing upward towards it. The sounds swell to a buzzing crescendo and then stabilize in a singular, vibrating tone. As gradually as the sounds emerged, they disappear into silence leaving thirteen bodies gently trembling, exhaling gentle sighs of completion. A cough cracked the silence and Raphael speaks.

"Open up the base of your spines now and begin inhaling up the Earth Energy through your first conduit. On the exhale, circulate this energy throughout your entire body. Stay with this cycle...of inhaling it up and circulating it throughout the body on the exhale until you reach your point of maximum density. Then, resume your chanting by resonating a sound to match the frequency of the Earth Energy inside your body. [Pausing] Get a sense of being an extension or, protuberance of the Earth...a bump on the planet...indivisible with the Earth and receptive to its vast support and stability. When this has stabilized, you've reached **bump-consciousness.**"

3

Time: *The Great Collapse*
Place: *PSI-Matrix Memory Bank, Planetary Limbic System*

Oh, how we love those little bumps...especially as they're arranged in circles. How else can the essences circulate and mix so well? In the midst of our evaluation of your progress, we are continually pleased with the steady emergence of these earth renewal rites and the humans who so graciously surrender themselves to them.

Some of these humans understand the tremendous magnitude and purpose of their current functions and as such, require more stabilization lest their buoyancy factor exceed their bump consciousness and they become as useless to us as kites cut free in an electrical thunderstorm.

As your prophets have said before you: **Many are called yet few are chosen.** *The business at hand is, of course, your point of maximum density. You have entered a stage lasting, your time between 1987 and 1992, where we can not work together unless your futile hankering for* clarity and perspective ceases. This does not mean that clarity is without purpose now. We are implying that your striving for it is getting in our way. The era of **ambitious clarity** is over. It lasted, your time, between 1964 and 1986 and accomplished its objective. We are now eliminating the clarity factor for those striving for it and introducing new degrees and levels of density.

Levels of density will be experienced, by your majority, as the human conditions of confusion, disorientation and bewilderment. Those who resist density, and there are many, will distort these natural conditions into forms of suffering, illness and catastrophe. The Warriors of Light amongst you will incorporate **density as a value** and use disorientation and turbulence as a gateway to your true potential state. What you really want to know is: **How dense can you get?**

4

Time: *Later that night*
Place: *At the base of Bell Rock in Sedona, Arizona*

The thirteen people seated in a circle gradually start moving...stretching muscles, flexing spines and voicing their return from the group trance of bump consciousness. Some of them stand, brushing off bits of dirt and dust gathered during the ceremony. A few remain seated and motionless, assimilating the Earth's transmission. Two others spontaneously start jumping up and down together while a third runs around the setting howling with joy. After several minutes of everybody more or less doing their own thing, they all gather seated in the circle again and a woman speaks up. "It seems like the Earth is really grieving tonight."

Raphael offers a mildly challenging look. "What do you mean 'grieving'?"

The woman struggles with her words. "She's hurting...she's crying out...to be healed...it was pretty...dense..."

He looks up at her. "I got something about density, too. Density as a value. You see, we tend to all get caught up in being, like totally, *clear* all the time and I think it's really starting to get in the way."

A ripple of self-conscious laughter circulates throughout the group. "No, really. I'm starting to see how all this bullshit striving for clarity is just more New Age cosmic foo foo."

A middle-aged longhair wearing a cowboy hat and brown, fringed jacket shakes his head. "No, no, no... I don't know about you, man, but I'm feeling pretty clear right now. What grandmother earth told me was, well...she said, 'Stay Loose, and don't you worry about a thing 'cause you're in the flow and that's where I want you.' So, there's no real problem, you see, it's only people that make the problem. Life's not a problem, man...people are..."

"Peace, bro'...but hey, don't be **too sure** man..."

A few laugh, while the longhair grows visibly defensive. "Look, Mister Word Twister...ain't nobody suffering no illusions around here except maybe...you."

"Yeah? Talk to me...what do you see, man?" He relaxes his stance a bit, takes a deep breath and a long, cold hard look at his new opponent.

The middle-aged longhair fixes his gaze on Raphael. "You may be right but that doesn't make it happen. To know it doesn't mean you're doing it. I just want you to **walk your talk,** man."

"Walk my talk...that's good...I'll just think about that...thanks..."

"Don't thank me, man, **and don't think about it** either. **Just...*do it.*"**

THE GODDESS GUILD

1

"The primary purpose of Goddess rituals is in generating a strong enough Feminine Vortex to attract more Gods to play with."
from THE GODDESS GAZETTE, Issue #22

Time: *Sunset, August 17, 1987*
Place: *10,000 feet above the Pacific outside LAX Airport, Los Angeles*

Nestled comfortably inside the spacious First Class section of the Boeing 747, Michael sits and reads the headlines of today's Los Angeles *Times*: **SECOND WORST AIR CATASTROPHE IN U.S. HISTORY!** He shakes his head. His mind reels and spins in a dizzy array of mixed emotions and fragmented symbolic associations: *Something's definitely out of sync here. If there's a higher order to this catastrophe, please god tell me what it is. Why are these things happening now? Why now? Maybe someone or something's trying to stop Harmonic Convergence from happening?! I wonder what Jose Arguelles thinks about all this. Maybe I'm supposed to contact him about our entrapped Sirius Star Princess. He probably already knows about this crash. What am I saying, man? Arguelles isn't going to want to talk with me...who am I? I mean, who do I think I am? We've probably already connected on the astral, anyway. Anything can happen...right? Right...*

"May I have your attention, please. The captain has informed us of unexpected turbulence before our final descent into Los Angeles International Airport. Please fasten your seat belts, place your seats in their upright position and extinguish all cigarettes. We should be arriving in LAX very shortly and...thank you for flying Trans World."

There's something she's not telling us. Holy shit, we're going to crash and burn! Everybody's so fucking calm, I can't believe it. Doesn't anybody else read between the lines around here? Maybe I should just get the story straight from the pilots. No, they'll think

I'm crazy and arrest me. Man O God O Man O God... I can just see this place vaporizing into a fireball... Is that a woman's face I see forming in the clouds? Please God, hear me now... Bring me within your loving heart. Protect me. Relieve my soul of its mortal coil before the blast hits. Please God, don't let me die inside a burning body...have mercy on my soul. Don't let me burn...

2

Time: *The Great Collapse*
Place: *Telempathic Media Services, SIRIUS STAR SYSTEM*

In Lake'ch, I am another yourself. The evolution of your mythology requires passage through three preliminary stages before this message can be registered. To help you absorb this transmission, we will now review the trinary circuit of your Mythic Intelligence as it's been constructed by the changing whole of your racial memory. The **animistic primary node** *of this trinary circuit enables your race to survive on this planet by identifying with the animals who came before you. This developed into the belief that spirits reside in all things—from minerals to vegetables to animals to places—and is responsible for your planetary self-preservation. Countless millennia later, with your technological advances,* **the integrative** *circuitry of a* **stellar mythos** *emerged with your awareness of the heavenly bodies enveloping your planet from the sky above and below you. After several ages, it reached its apotheosis during your current stage, which is known to us as* **The Great Collapse.** *In this end period, manmade satellites, rudimentary spacecraft and primitive radar instruments have been sent up and out into interplanetary orbit to expand what you believe to be your future purpose on this planet:* **outer space exploration.**

As each previous node on this trinary mythic circuit has formed from irreversible errors in human judgement, so the final **transmitter** *node is now being structured amidst a continuum of aerial catastrophes. These human sucrifices will continue until an* **interstellar mythos** *stabilizes amongst the eleventh percentile responsible for triggering your evolutionary leaps. Your status as candidates for interstellar membership* is initiated with the absolute integrity resultant from complete identification with your own **wave forms**...the totality of your individual energetic fields. You are stars in formation. This star information has been brought to you by your non-local media services courtesy of the Sirius Star System. Your local program now resumes...

3

Time: *Sunset, August 17, 1987*
Place: *Malibu Hills, 800 feet above the California Coast*

    The Goddess Guild is cloistered away inside a large, well-lit architect's dream house hovering precariously atop a hill overlooking the ocean. Its three floors and five bedrooms provide the five "inside" women who maintain the Guild a haven for their mission. As the Goddess Guild, these women continue training "outsiders" in accepting their natural birthrights as goddesses by initiation into Level One ceremonies occurring every new moon morning. Here, thirteen women meet wearing leafy wreaths and white togas to sing, dance and frolic on the grassy hillside overlooking the Guild. Then, every full moon night, thirteen initiated goddesses gather together around a small fire under the moonlight to chant, sing and howl their hearts out. Between moons, the women who do not live in the house rarely meet save for the occasional sunset ceremonies assembling them together.

    Today's sunset...all twenty-six women lay in a circle on the northwest slope of the hillside, garbed in wreaths and togas. This ceremony is dedicated to the marriage between the Sun and the Earth. All twenty-six lay on their backs, their heads touching...pointing towards a small central circle...like petals of a flower. The unfolding beauty of their symmetry failed to contain the mirthful giggles now rippling throughout their ritual ground design. As they lay there, all breathed deep and then sang...sweet wordless melodies of gratitude...from the earth to the sun...from the sun to the earth...and then, the words formed:

> *Father Sun, Mother Earth*
> *For what it's worth,*
> *We give our bodies to the Earth*
> *To sing our song of mirth…your sweet song of Birth…*

> *Father Earth, Mother Sun*
> *Look what we have done,*
> *We gave our hearts to the Sun*
> *Just to feed the one we love…the one we love…*

Inside the small central circle of heads stood hunched a wiry, elderly man in his late seventies. With his arms outstretched slightly upward and his face towards the setting sun, his fragile body quaked and trembled while tears of joy filled his eyes. He started singing…a song he sang many times before as a young boy…a song of praise to women and wine and song. A song his father taught him the day the boy's mother died…a song they sang together many times to pass the agony of their loss. As the women's singing grew in resonance, it cadenced into multiple levels of sonic texture at his feet. The elder man's body gradually collapsed down into itself, murmuring softly as he fell. All the women, one by one…like plucking petals, rose…creating a space for the falling man. He nods faintly as he crumbles to the earth crying his mother's name.

4

Time: *2:30 PM, September 7, 1987*
Place: *The Phoenix Bookstore in Santa Monica, Southern California*

The bookstore is vacant, save for the tremendous array and sheer volume of metaphysical archives layering each and every wall from floor to ceiling. The owners, a father and son, are gone today. Their store manager is in the back room drinking black coffee while checking the computer for a rare book on the practice of sexual magick. In through the front door of the store walks the wiry frame of the now vibrant, enthusiastic Michael who looks around at the books, bewildered and disoriented.

"Hello…anybody home?" The manager ignores the call and continues scanning the screen for sex magick…then, "C" for Crowley. "I guess not…what a ghost town. What a place!"

The store manager soon emerges from behind the back wall door and walks toward the north wall looking for his book. "What can I do for you?"

"I'm new in town. Quite an amazing little place you've got here." Business pretty slow today, heh?"

The store manager looks him up and down with sarcasm. "Heh…where have you been?"

Michael entire face beams. "Bali…"

The manager looks away and then back at him. "Gorgeous place, Bali. Say, I suppose you've heard about the Harmonic Convergence…"

Michael steps toward the counter while the other man stoops down to file a book away. "Sure have. What do you think is really going on?" The man's head peers back over the counter's edge. "Sold several cases of his book in just two weeks and then, poof! Haven't sold one copy since August 15th…deadest thing I've ever seen around here. It's like everybody just up and died. I don't know what to think yet. It's hard to tell with prophecy until time proves it one way or another. I know we could've used more books but his publisher backordered the damn thing and nobody could get copies when everybody wanted them. Publishers do that sometimes…"

Michael's head bobs up and down. "Maybe they got greedy or something."

They both look at each other in the silence. "Or something…"

Michael shrugs and then, looks blankly out the door to the empty street beyond. "This may sound strange…"

The manager laughs. "No, it won't…"

"…but I think I missed the Harmonic Convergence. I was all set up for it and then, there was this…"

The manager laughs again. "You, too? I didn't feel a thing myself."

Michael turns abruptly to him, an urgency in his eyes. "You don't understand…it's not that I didn't feel anything, I did. It was real peaceful…even serene, like the calm before a storm…even magical…"

The manager's eyes roll up into his shaking head just as a woman enters the store…a thirtyish, red-haired woman in a military green jumpsuit. Her sea-green eyes gently sparkle as she approaches the men, whose attention she completely magnetizes. A soft yet strident bounce camouflages her almost disconcertingly sweet voice as she speaks. "Hello boys…do you have, uh…ummm…**SEX AND DRUGS** by…Robert Anton Wilson? I believe it's been reissued on, ummmmm….Falcon Press."

The manager stutters. "What a co-coincidence… I was just looking for that book not twenty minutes ago and found our last copy. It's yours if you want it! With synchronicity like this, I think Bob Wilson would probably want you to have it, too…"

"Thank goddess…you boys look a little down in the dumps. You won't let this **post-convergence dead zone** get to you, will you? You know it'll only get a lot worse before it gets any better. Maybe you ought to meet up with some real rowdy Harmonica Virgins and have yourselves a wild party or something…"

Michael's eyes widen with amazement then, immediately sharpen their focus. "Get worse? What do you mean, **worse**?"

She pulls out a hundred-dollar bill from her purple purse and gives it to the manager, whose disgruntled expression informs her that he doesn't have change. She looks into her purse again and pulls out a fifty, offering that instead. **"When the Light hits, the Dark gets tough**. We'll be underground assimilating until mid-February or so is my guess. Just check the Ephemeris to see when Saturn and Uranus are conjunct."

The manager rings up the book and returns her change while watching her breathe. "Assimilating what?"

Pocketing the change inside her jumpsuit front lapel pocket, she looks straight into his eyes with sincere but utter disbelief. "Light, silly…"

Michael barely contains his excitement and, without thinking, begins walking away with her as she turns to go. She turns to him. "Until a lady invites his company, a man best consider himself safe and alone."

Michael stops in his tracks, smiling and obviously embarrassed. "I'd like to talk with you. And, I don't know how. I've never met someone like you before and...that's not just another line."

A cunning smile etches across her lips. "I know... I can see that. There's nothing inherently wrong about feeding a woman lines, by the way."

Michael takes a deep breath and walks toward her. "Wanna go out?"

She laughs, while gently chiding him. "Sure, if you don't mind tagging along with me for a few errands first."

He shrugs. "No, I don't mind...your car or mine?"

She pulls her keys out of her purse. "Mine, preferably...don't worry... I'll return you in one piece...promise."

He continues his meandering nonchalance. "That's OK. I don't worry anymore and...I never accept promises..."

She looks at him for one, long, lingering moment. "Wonderful... I'll hold you to it, too. My car's the silver one over there..."

Astonished, Michael's jaw drops slightly. "The BMW?!"

She delights in correcting him. "The Mercedes."

As they both get into the car and pull away, a coffee-colored Cadillac moves into their previous parking space blasting Chuck Berry's *Johnny B. Goode*. Its elderly, black male driver starts laughing loud and long as he notices the bumper sticker on the rear chrome of the exiting Mercedes. **"I brakedance for animals...** I gotta remember that..." He laughs and laughs and laughs...

5

Time: *The Great Collapse*
Place: *LIVE from the Pleiades!!! The Intergalactic Comedy Hour...*

In Lake'ch, I am another yourself. Laughter is the most direct route to God...filling your meaningless human heads with Light. By virtue of planetary arrangement, certain human lights are brought *together via **synchronicity**. Here at the Pleiades, synchronicity is the standard time zone and an outlet for your **planetary humor**. Every time the Earth laughs, mega-photons are released and immediately circulated throughout its surface crust magnetizing certain human males and females together. Here and there, human men and women discover their threshold for **deep and meaningless illumination**. Too much meaning darkens the human light and compels the lifelong spiritual quest for a good laugh. Many are called but few are chosen due to the inability of the many to **laugh real hard and long**. If you are siriusly considering a career in planetary service, you'd best start laughing real hard and real long. This is no joke, dahlink. We love you more than you think...more than you'd even care to imagine...*

6

Time: *Sunset, September 7, 1987*
Place: *Inside a silver Mercedes, up the Pacific Coast Highway, Malibu*

After hours of impassioned conversation, the red-haired woman and Michael abruptly enter a dead-end lull. Suddenly, neither has anything to say to the other. The heavy silence discomforts the woman yet she knows how important it is to her position in the ensuing evening's activities. Michael is simply relieved **not** to talk. He needs time now to assimilate what he feels is the most extraordinary coincidence of his life...of meeting, what he believes to be, the woman of his dreams. The wheels turn and spin in his head like the polished chrome hubcaps of her Mercedes as she turns the wheel east, starting the long, steep climb up to the Goddess Guild.

After stuffing a cassette tape into the stereo, she glances over to him. "You know, Michael...I just realized that during our long talk I never told you my name...even after you told me yours... and that you've never asked. That takes a certain kind of internal security and I like that in a man."

Michael's entire face lit up as he continued looking at her. "What is your name, anyway?"

She studies him carefully before answering. "It's not...anyway." They both laugh together. "It's Arielle."

His eyes shine. "Arielle...sounds ancient. What does it mean?" She pauses then, licks her full lips. "It is. It means *the revealer*...Ariel is one of the four Archangels..." She steadies her gaze and looks directly into Michael's dilated left pupil, while an ultraviolet spark travels between them.

He jumps slightly in his seat. "Hey, what! What are you doing?!"

She looks back to the road in front of her. "Just checking you out. You're ripe Michael...have you just separated from a lady recently?"

Astonished, Michael looks at her long and hard. "Yes. How could you tell?"

"Your shields are broken and you've been blown wide open. You've been unraveled and left undone, Michael. It's really quite the opportunity, you know. You're vulnerable enough now to really start rewiring some of that outdated circuitry...especially around sex, power and women." Michael's chest contracts slightly into a defensive position. "Before you even think about defending yourself, you might wish to take a deep breath and relax. I'm actually on your side."

Michael inhales and relaxes his torso. "Your right. What... what do you mean by rewiring my circuitry..."

She looks at him with a child-like smile and moon-illumined eyes. Your central neural system..."

Michael interrupts her. "Neural?"

She continues. "If given a choice between having a *nervous* or a **neural** system, which would you opt for?"

He thinks for a moment. "Neural...of course."

"As I was saying, your central neural system is deadened in those areas where you have accepted culturally and socially conditioned programs, or definitions, of a given reality in lieu of direct neural engagement in these areas."

Michael's brow perplexes. "Do you talk normal?"

Her lips tighten slightly into a cool disdain. "For example, if reading *Playboy* magazines as a boy kept turning you onto a certain "look" in a woman then...you would have to find a woman replicating that look before you were sexually fulfilled. Now, imagine a world of women unassociated with any images whatsoever. In this world, you'd only find out what turned you on by experiencing each and every one directly, for the very first time, without any previous program to go on. Is that normal enough for you?"

Michael watches the passing roadside, uncertain as to whether he should ask her to stop the car and let him out or to jump on her bones. "A world without images...how can that be possible?"

Arielle notices his now obvious discomfort. "Well there are three images we conjure up in Goddess Training...kind of like training wheels or handles...until we're more secure in our basic womanhood to not need any of them exclusively anymore."

Michael calms down and looks at her. "Yeah? What are they?"

"Every woman is free to be Persephone, Demeter and Hecate... the holy feminine trinity. We are all maiden, mother and crone. It's so beautiful, really..."

"Hecate is the crone?"

She confirms his statement with a somber tone. "Yes, Hecate is the crone."

Michael studies her profile. "I hope you don't mind if I say that you don't look like a crone...to me."

She grins widely. "That's because tonight...I am the crone."

His eyebrows arch, surprised. "Tonight? Hmmm...and what, pray tell, am I tonight?"

"That depends entirely on you. Just as I have invited you into my company, so have you invited me into yours. With your permission, I will initiate you into the mysteries of your own soul."

"You're going to initiate me?"

She nods, slowly. "With your permission. Yes. Now, you didn't think you'd be coming home with a real live goddess and escape initiation, did you?!" She glances over at his forlorn expression.

"Don't look so worried...true initiation engages everybody. I'll be initiated, too, into a new level...with you and...your anima."

He ponders a moment. "My inner feminine spirit..."

She sighs with relief. "Very good, Michael...you see, it's no accident that we've met. As I see it, we can offer each other something of **real value** tonight or get into the usual boy-girl robotics. You choose."

"Boy-girl robotics?" He laughs." That's a good one."

Her tone grows severe yet seductive. "Now what's it going to be...initiation into the Feminine mysteries, or robots in love?" He laughs nervously. "What a choice! No other alternatives?" She shakes her head with a smile. "OK...let's see what's behind...Feminine mysteries."

She looks at him while shaking her index finger in mock scolding. "No personality worship, OK? Nobody falls in love with anybody and everybody keeps their noses clean, got it?!"

Michael gasps. "I got it, I got it..."

Arcturus twinkles mercilessly from above the western horizon behind them. The silver Mercedes sidewinds up and around the serpentine path to the top of a hill where it turns south, rolling silently down along the ridge overlooking the rapidly darkening sea. Unseen by them, on the other side of the hill, hangs suspended the very full moon. The Mercedes turns around the bend and they see it together. Looking at each other in the cool stillness of the moon's silver light, Michael comments. "Some moon, huh?!"

Arielle smiles, wistful and expectant, the moonlight reflecting easily off her rapidly glazing eyes. "Pisces Moon...the Dakini Moon..."

Michael responds, excitedly. "I'm a Pisces..."

"...then you, Michael are one very lucky fish..."

7

Time: *The Great Collapse*
Place: *Telempathic Media Services, SIRIUS STAR SYSTEM*

We interrupt this program to bring you the following Interstellar News Update. There are now definitive signs of an interstellar mythos emerging in your planet's central neural systems, causing upset in the established, governing minds of the Old Guard. Synapse fires and neurotransmitter chemical spillage have already taken its toll on the outdated circuitry of the global brain, while world religions continue working overtime to maintain moral odor.

*Interstellar ambassadors from Pleiades claim responsibility for stabilizing the trinary circuit of Mythic Intelligence in the human species. Through the Entertainment Industry, Consciousness Technologies and the camouflaged, galvanizing force of humor, these spiritual vigilantes work unseen behind the smokescreen of this rapidly expanding socio-economic tendency humans call The New Age Movement. It seems there is now a definite interference established to slow down the current harvest cycle of the Great Collapse. Keep your antennae unwrapped, as News Update remains on the scene to give you the story **first**. You are stars in formation. This star information has been brought to you by your non-local media services courtesy of the Sirius Star System. Your local program will now resume...*

8

Time: *Monday Night, Labor Day, September 7, 1987*
Place: *THE GODDESS GUILD, Malibu Hills, California*

Michael sits alone on the white leather couch in the spacious and very white living room of the Goddess Guild. The undecipherable sounds of women talking and laughing two rooms over unsettle him. He twists and turns, arching his back and cracking his knuckles, and then leafs through a high fashion magazine on the marble table. A few minutes later Arielle silently enters the room from behind. She stops several yards away and watches him read…gazing softly at the space around his body. After a few moments, she sings a soft gentle wordless melody. Michael lifts his eyes from the magazine and looks straight ahead, taking in the enveloping quality of her voice.

She slowly walks to him, hands outstretched, as he gradually places the magazine down on his lap, raising his arms into the air…yielding to her hands…as they touch his own. "Very nice, Michael, very beautiful, intuitive man…" She bends down and kisses him lightly on the lips. "Let's talk."

Walking around the enormous white couch, she seats herself in the white, canvas director's chair across from him. Through the cathedral windows, the view of the moon bounces off the distant sea behind her. Both look at each other in anticipation.

She sees the magazine on his lap and laughs. "One of our goals is advertising The Goddess Guild in *Cosmopolitan*. Our version of the initiatory rites of Isis involve three very contemporary gates, or prerequisites: a college degree, financial independence and natural beauty."

Michael laughs, uneasily. "How do you evaluate natural beauty?"

"We don't. What's natural is obvious and known by women everywhere. It's the first two gates that really concern us. Their acquisition separates the chaff from the grain in that a certain degree of intellectual and economic strength is inseparable from true liberation for today's woman. We're not saying that women can't be or aren't goddesses if they're financially dependent or conceptually vacant. It's just that…"

He cuts in. "What are you saying then?"

Her face tenses effortlessly, masking the exasperation inside her. "All we're saying is that there are certain prerequisites to the Guild…to our particular women's group. Every magic circle has its gates and these are ours. Enough of me and the Guild. Let's talk about me and you…us."

Michael grows visibly defensive and agitated. "Why? I mean, what are those women doing right now? Where are they and how come we can't even hear them Are they listening to us now?"

Her eyes roll up into her head as she laughs and then stops, abruptly. "You men...so self-important and suspicious. The goddesses are out on the hillside preparing the space for tonight's full moon ceremony, like they do every full moon. I've invited you to participate only if you **wish to. Don't worry**...nobody's going to force you to do anything around here." She laughs again, realizing the absurdity of her words. "Would you like to join us, Michael?"

He nervously maintains eye contact and nods. "Yes. I wish to join the ceremony. What are your prerequisites, or gates, for me since I'm obviously not a woman?"

She laughs again, this time, with Michael and not at him. Both stop laughing together. "Oh, yes you are, Michael. You enter the temple by your willingness to be instructed by a priestess. You may enter the ceremony only through the gate of your anima. Fortunately for us, I am a priestess and...your anima is more than ripe for the picking. In fact, it's rotting on the ground." Both laugh.

His eyebrows furrow. "Us? Why fortunate for us?"

She purses her lips for a moment. "Any initiation remains incomplete until everybody ascends together. One way my ascension occurs is through initiating men to their internal feminine... their anima. That, my friend, is no small task. You see, most men are for the most part, **wilderbeasts,** and only few ever rise to the occasion of their humanity. Fewer still ascend to their godhood and even then, they can only be expected to be **part-time gods at best."**

Michael shrugs. "Then, why do it?"

A trace of melancholy joins her sigh. "To bring men and women together. A goddess seeks a man whose anima is preparing for its next evolutionary leap. When a man is ready to be instructed by a woman about his own internal feminine, he has been accepted into the Temple of the Goddess. Do you still wish to enter the temple?"

He nods. "Yes."

Arielle remains silent, intuiting for reluctance in his reply. "After coming inside, there's really no turning back. Do you still wish to enter the adept ceremony of the goddesses?"

Without a trace of hesitation, Michael responds. "Yes, I do."

Both sigh with relief as she walks over and hugs him. "Beautiful, beautiful man..." They look into each other's eyes as Michael kisses her gently on her lips. After one full moment, she pulls away while pressing his hand to her breast.

Michael's eyes soften as he responds. "I'm all yours...where to?" She takes this hand and leads him down to sit on the plush white carpet in the open area beneath a sixty-gallon, tropical saltwater aquarium. "These fish come from several differing oceans of the world, yet they all get along with each other. Aren't they beautiful? I want you to watch them. Watch them closely as if you're inside the tank with them. Then, enter the tank...project your consciousness inside and become the water. While you do this, I will speak with your anima."

Michael steadies his gaze on the multi-colored, subterranean seaworld. Arielle stands up and turns out all the lights, leaving Michael's mind free to roam inside the aquarium's internal illumination. She sits down again across the room from him, closing her eyes. Upon opening them, a soft white light rises from inside her heart and radiates out her eyes and beyond her into the space around Michael's body.

Her soothing, hypnotic voice speaks to his depths. "That's right. Settle into it. Become the water, Michael...be the water. Transfer your feeling to the water." Michael's eyes water now as his body grows slightly rigid. "That's right, be the water... Now... let the fish breathe you in...let the fish breathe you in...feel them inside you as they breathe you in. Pass through them and into yourself. Good." Arielle closes her eyes and takes three deep breaths, tears now rolling down her cheeks. She takes three more deep breaths and opens her eyes again. "Michael...come back now...feel your feet...feel your feet, Michael...wiggle your toes and you'll come home."

Michael's eyes widen and then, squint shut and then widen open again. "My legs are asleep...what a trip..."

She calls for him across the room. "What did you see, Michael?"

He attempts to stretch his legs and starts massaging them. She gets up, moves closer to him and starts massaging his feet. "What did I see…it wasn't seeing so much as I guess…I mean, I saw the fish when I was the water and all but it wasn't really seeing so much as, uh, feeling and seeing, at the same time…if that makes any sense?"

"Yes, it does…go on…" She continues massaging his feet.

"Oh, that feels good…don't stop, OK? I'm kind of spacing out around it right now. How extraordinarily beautiful those fish are. Aquariums…at least like this one…they're like crystal balls… gateways to other dimensions…entirely! By the way, did you talk to my anima?"

She shakes her head in mock pity. "Yes. And it doesn't look good. Just what I was afraid of, really. No need to worry, though. And…she's more than willing to come out and play with the goddesses tonight. It's just that she is rather young, petulant and, perhaps most of all…**spiritually pissed.** Quite a haughty little bitch…" Arielle works hard to contain her laughter.

Michael smiles. "Young? What do you mean? How young?"

She laughs wildly then, catches herself. "Oh, about the going age, shape and look of your average monthly *Playboy* centerfold… Uh, you know…**young?**"

Michael nods his head. "Oh, yeah…**young.**"

VERTICAL STABILITY

1

"The waking process is much like a connect-the-dots game. However, if Humankind does not first become vertically connected, then it will not have sufficient awareness and understanding to connect the dots, much less to even know what the dots are."
DR. ACTARA TREADWELL, Extraterrestrial Ambassador

Time: *The Great Collapse*
Place: *The High Court Council of CHAPEL PERILOUS*

Ominos...dominos...eye, nose and ears know...NOBODY KNOWS... In Lake'ch, I am another yourself. Order in the court! There's an odor in the court! Welcome...welcome to Chapel Perilous! This is a most extraordinary gathering of lost souls. Why, you all look like you've just missed the bus headed for the **1991 Materialists' Convention** and...indeed, **you have**. Corporate mongers, Wall Street kamikaze traders and other useful idiots...welcome! You are all here on trial for the same reason and that is this: through your horizontal, material identification you have left mercifully little space in your human forms for a living soul.

Your passionate deification of the external planes has assured the complete **destabilization** of your internal **vertical connection**. Since it is a **luciferian crime** to turn your back on the Creator, you'll remain here in the timeless, spaceless limbo of Chapel Perilous...until a vertical stability affords your re-entry into the human forms awaiting you. Your verdict is to hang in suspense, not knowing whether or not it is too late to return. Where exactly you shall be placed by the Creator shall be *determined by the stature of the individual crimes against your true nature. In the meantime, the jury hangs in suspense.*

2

Time: *7:17 PM, September 7, 1987*
Place: *Room 230, Boulderama Hotel, Boulder, COLORADO*

Gabrielle sits comfortably in the antique red, cushioned chair across from Raphael who sits, eyes closed, on a small Americana-style love seat. She gazes out the window to her left while his eyes flutter up inside his head, a rapturous smile animating his face. Other than his eyes and mouth, there is no movement in the room. The stillness expands from his own deepening, internal calm until his voice breaks the silence...catching her immediate attention.

"Spiritually, you're as dead as a Tibetan doornail, Gabrielle. Your life has reached a point of epic stagnation and the inertia you feel now is the result of years and years of literally outdoing yourself. You're royally stuck."

Gabrielle tensed then, took a breath before speaking. "What do you mean by 'outdoing myself'?"

"You're a real go-getter...you get your way for the most part and pretty much attain whatever you set your mind to. In the long run, this has had the unfortunate side-effect of a kind of frustration leaving you feeling numb and isolated. Your internal reaction to this predicament has been to start seeking a truer experience of love because everything you've loved up to this point has been all used up. The relationship you're in tells me that. Your job does, too. You're even starting to outgrow your close friends. Now, the way outdoing works goes like this. You're a 'doer.' You do what you do real well. Every time you succeed in doing anything that well, the side-effect of your effectiveness creates a psychic shield around your aura…something others pick up as an 'edge' about you. As these shields accumulate, they shut out new information and something vital gets trapped inside. It's like a break in your oxygen supply…you die, or rather, your spirit atrophies."

She turns her gaze to the window while absorbing his message, sorting out what resonates to be true from the rest. She watches the sun-painted cumulus clouds drift by through the panoramic twilight sky. "It's all true so far…keep going."

He sighs. "Lucky for you, lucky for me. You're intelligent enough to not fight it, which at this point would be absolutely pointless and a waste of our time. Since you're dead, spiritually speaking, you've entered an extremely fertile phase of your process…a time where you can literally look forward to a new life and, especially, a new expression of love. That is, if you're willing to die a little."

She laughs softly for a moment. "I thought I was already dead. What do you mean by 'die a little'?"

"Give it expression…ritualize it…get it out of your system by finding a form for its expression…like…give yourself a funeral…or, have someone do it for you…or, just find a time and space in your life to suffer, drop and die. You see, you're in a **molting phase** right now. Like a snake shedding its skin, you've got to find some private place to do some major shedding."

Gabrielle's eyes glaze over in mild shock. "A funeral?!"

He chuckles with apprehension. "Don't be so literal, Gabrielle. **A living funeral**…one that gives you complete permission to die psychologically, so you can collapse and get on with it. It's a personal ritual. Are you open to personal rituals?"

She looks straight at him, the pupils in her eyes expanding into circular black pools. "Yes, I think I am. I mean, I haven't had any formal training in this kind of thing…"

He suddenly opens his eyes, interrupting her. "All the better. Just find a space or room where you're not going to be interrupted for several hours. Then, gather some collapsing music…you know, sounds and songs you can easily fall apart around. If you wish, light some candles and burn some incense…read appropriate poetry. Do anything you like to have fun with it and remember, rebirth always accompanies the death of the old. The big positive comes out of the big black…negative."

She glances out the window. "I think I know what you mean…" He laughs, loud and forceful. "Think? You've got enough intuition to put off thinking for the rest of the year. It's just that you opt out for conventional excuses like feigning ignorance when you really know the score. Once you get into the habit of believing the very thing that's actually happening to you, you'll know what I mean."

She looks back at him. "You're right. So what if I don't want to get into ritual in order to…die. What are my other alternatives?"

He considers, then deliberates an answer. "I don't know if you can avoid ritual at this point but I suppose any excursion into an exotic terrain will do."

"Like take a trip?"

"If your destination doesn't discourage your cracking shell. It's not the best time to visit your family…or, for that matter, friends that have come to know and love your shell. If you do take a trip, it's probably best to be around someone that'll allow you the space to get into marginal states or…go somewhere you've never been, so nobody has any expectations of you whatsoever."

"Marginal states?"

"Sorry…marginal…hmmm…OK. You've entered a genuine initiation rite of passage and your first phase has begun. That's the isolation…detachment…and overall sense of disconnectedness you've been feeling. That's level one. Level two involves marginal states of being…where you're feeling neither here nor there…not quite out of the old and not knowing enough about where you're going to make choices. Marginal kind of means limbo. It's like being **between** personalities almost, and it reeks of rootless flux."

"I think I'm already feeling marginal...the indecision thing. I've been having the hardest time making choices and that's not normal for me. Can you tell me anything about...level three? What exactly am I in for?"

He chuckles again, catching her off guard and she laughs, too. "Exactly? That's rich. I don't know how exact you want to hear it. It might throw you off, considering you haven't **destabilized** enough to get through level two yet."

Still laughing, Gabrielle takes a deep breath. "I see your point. Well...how much do you want to tell me at this time?" He laughs, then suddenly stops and raises his hand, palm faced toward her solar plexus...his eyes fluttering up into his head.

"Hmmm...not much, really. If I had to say something about your future it's that there's a certain inevitability factor around meeting a man with whom you'll share an immediate and all-encompassing attraction with. But, he's not your regular soul-mate kind of guy. It's really quite different than that. You'll be brought together by virtue of your coinciding molting phases, so it'll have the emotion of 'destiny' to it. Don't get your hopes up, though. Synchronicity isn't everything..."

3

Time: 8:32 PM September 7, 1987
Place: *On a hillside overlooking the Goddess Guild, Malibu Hills*

Twelve young, middle-aged and elderly women in white togas stand around a crackling fire chanting, while metronomically clapping their hands in the twilight. A thirteenth climbs the hill towards them, leading another red-clad figure by the hand. Their two silhouettes cast the illusion of animated porcelain figurines crossing an opaque, illuminated landscape. They stop about two-thirds of the way, and Arielle turns to face her partner.

"Michael, stay here until you get the signal from us. While you're waiting, pray…pray to Hecate, the Goddess of Death…ask to be accepted by Her and offer her a specific deed you will do for…**all women**. But only offer the deed you are willing and able to follow through on, **no matter how small it is.** This is the most important part…that you *follow through on your deed,* lest you grow subject to Her wrath. She works best with respect. Got it?"

Michael nods his head in silence, and then coughs. Arielle kisses him on the forehead, on each cheek and on his left hand which she then places gently upon her chest. "Your name is Persephone. When we are ready to receive you, we will chant your name and, only then, are you invited to join us." She turns away without saying good-bye, walking up the hill in a rapid, steady gait.

Michael bends down on his knees, prostrating himself. The indigo sky darkens quickly as he mumbles his prayer to Hecate. "Oh, man oh god oh man oh god oh… Goddess of death…I've never prayed to you before. What do I say? How do I do it? I **know** you who you are. It was you I saw in the sky from my airplane window…it was your face in the clouds. It was you who guided the pilot to a safe landing and it is you to whom I thank for meeting Arielle and bringing me here. I wish to heal my soul and I have been asked to dedicate a deed to you. I vow…to stop buying *Playboy* magazines…in fact, I vow to stop contaminating my mind with any images that make women objects. I wish to know women for who they are and how I can serve them. Above all, I wish…"

Interrupted by distant chanting, Michael sits up and gazes bleary-eyed across the upward slope to the glowing fire circle above.

"Per-se-pho-nee… Per-se-pho-nee… Per-se-pho-nee…"

The chanting continues. He rises, tripping over his long, red velvet dress as he tries to stand. He rises again, straightening his gown and arranging his wig of long blond hair while walking up the hill towards the fire circle. Moments later he comes upon the surrounding aura of the fire's light. The rhythm of the goddess' chant gradually synchronizes with each step Michael takes. His heavily made-up, lipsticked and mascaraed face absorbs the moonlight...reflecting into the black night like a geisha mask afloat in Texas oil. His walk wobbles slightly, yet he persists forward to the illuminated goddess circle, where they continue chanting...with greater intensity and the cadences of a sing-song round:

"Per-se-pho-nee... Per-se-pho-nee... Per-se-pho-nee..."

Michael stops a few feet away from the circle, faintly swaying to the rhythm of their sounds, now with both eyes closed and mouth dropped open. The goddesses continue singing while breaking their circle to envelop him. Now, from all directions, Michael hears his new inner name swirling throughout around his head, into his heart and down throughout his entire body. He sways and rocks with the chant, breathing harder and deeper, tears starting to fill his line-smeared eyes. The chant then stops abruptly, while Michael continues swaying and rocking in its wake. Arielle's voice sounds forth. "Persephone...Hecate speaks. Goddess is below you embedded in the earth. Breathe Her up into yourself, then invite her inside your womb where She can **feed you. Become Her**...and no matter what happens, keep breathing. Stay with Her and She will stay with you."

4

Time: *The Great Collapse*
Place: *SIRIUS TV—Channel 23; MEDIUMSHIP UPDATE!!!*

In Lake'ch...I am another yourself. Trance Mediumship has been your planet's historical method of heralding spiritual currents into its mainstream societies. Lightworkers are crossing the Great Channel during this time to absorb the **shock of disconnection** essential for triggering your next social mutation. Prostitution has been your planet's hysterical method for dispersing valuable spiritual information during the more oppressive cycles of civilization. As channelers and prostitutes alike are both paid to give their bodies over to a foreign entity, together they form an incubating polarity. The Channeling phenomenon is a side-effect of a massive sexual crisis now resulting from the short-circuiting neo-puritan, socio-moral programming in most central nervous systems of the Western World. On the genetic front, channeling expresses a sophisticated style of panic often accompanying the distinct awareness of potential species extinction. **Your world is on fire and its people are looking for an exit.** Our Entity-On-The-Scene has the full report and it looks like...yes, it is...it looks like **the door is on the floor.** This has been a Channel 23 Update from your SIRIUS TV Networkers. **Stay tuned!**

5

Time: *8:12 PM September 7, 1987*
Place: *Room 230, Boulderama Hotel, Boulder COLORADO*

Gabrielle is looking out into the night, drying her teary eyes with hotel toilet tissue. After two deep sighs and a half-choked laugh, she looks back at Raphael who is sitting deadstill with both hands on his lap. "OK...I'm ready now, it's just that I

Vertical Stability

had to…I didn't know there was so much that's gone unspoken inside me and it's a bit much…"

His tone is consoling yet firm. "No problem…glad you're strong enough to bounce back. Shall we?"

She nods. "Yes…it can't get any worse, can it?"

He laughs. "You do have your sense of humor intact, don't you?" She laughs while crying her last few tears. "Yes, I think so…why?" He raises his left hand in the air, scanning her lower torso and pelvic region while she sighs, heavily. "How would you like become vertically stabilized?"

Her face grows quizzical. "Vertically stabilized? Sounds like vertigo…"

He shakes his head. "It's not. It's just a way to release foreign energy from your various internal systems…psychic contracts, cords and other energetic agreements keeping you out of present time and out of touch with your own, unique wave form. I wouldn't ask except you're psychic enough to do it on your own. You just lack the mechanical information."

She nods, looking straight ahead at him. "Yeah, let's do it. What do I need to know?"

"OK. First, center yourself. While you do that, I'll raise my energy a few notches…" Both gather themselves inward while he flutters his eyes up into his head…a tiny, blissful smile moving his lips. "OK…Gabrielle. This is the initiation of vertical stability. Our intention is to temporarily disconnect you from all horizontal obligations, resistances and addictions. Horizontal means anything of the world around you…other people, industry, money… the whole world game. You are temporarily disconnecting from your horizontal source in the surrounding world to reconnect more thoroughly with your vertical source of the stars above and the earth below. Are you clear with this intention and, if so, are you willing to go through with it?"

Gabrielle clasps her hands tightly together. "Yes…on both accounts."

"Good. Here we go. Settle your energy down through the vertical axis of your spinal column so that it completely envelops it. I'm assuming you're familiar with the locations of the chakras in your body?"

Her eyes closed, she nods. "Pretty much. If not, I'll ask."

"Terrific. Rest your attention in the center of your brain. From here scan downwards to the lower centers. Look at your root chakra...at the base of your spine. Look to see if there are any cords of light coming into there from the outside. If you see any, raise your hand. These are 'grounding contracts'...where you are literally keeping somebody else alive or stabilizing someone else's energy Big Time."

"What if no cords are coming in, but one is going out from inside me?"

"That means you are depending on someone else to ground you...to maintain security. If you are ready, very gently pull that cord...that security demand...pull it back and reconnect it down into the earth below you. Breathe into this."

"Oh my god...that's a relief...why didn't I think of that before?"

"It's too obvious. Now, breathe the earth's energy into your first center...that's right. Breathe it on in. When you're ready to move on, scan the second center just below the navel for any outgoing or incoming cords...the incoming are emotional demands from others...for you to feel their pain, pleasure and attraction. Outgoing cords are your demands. When you're ready, gently pull theirs out and pull your own cords back. Once again, with every release...breathe, and then breathe in earth energy into that center to heal the gap left behind."

"What a mire...it's like the plague in there..."

"Quite astute. Just keep breathing... Your circulating breath mobilizes the inertias and break up the frozen energy... See for yourself..."

She breathes deep and steady several times, nodding her head. "You're right. It's moving...uh oh, I'm feeling kind of nauseous now..."

"Keep breathing...exhale the excess drek down into the earth and then, inhale the earth up into this center. Whatever you do, don't hold your breath. Stay with it...keep breathing...but stay with it...let the earth in..."

6

Time: *9:43 PM, September 7, 1987*
Place: *A hillside fire circle, overlooking the Goddess Guild, Malibu Hills*

"Stay with it...let the earth fill you...you are the earth... you are the Goddess...you are a single, fluttering eyelash in Her left eye as She lifts her gaze to the stars. Invite the stars into your eyes, Persephone." Michael lifts his head and slowly opens his tear-flooded eyes to the night sky. The goddesses hold hands and gently sway, side to side, singing their song to Persephone. A small rapturous smile opens Michael's lips as he absorbs the illumination from the Pleiades star system transmitting directly from above...entering his optical fibres from light years away...

> *Per-se-pho-nee... Per-se-pho-nee... Per-se-pho-neeeeee...*
> *You are light, you are spring, you bring us everything...*
> *You are light, you are green, you bring us everything...*
> *You are light, you are dream, you bring us everything...*
> *You are light, you are seen, you bring us everything...*

everything Persephone…everything Persephone…everything Persephone
everything Persephone…everything Persephone…everything Persephone
everything Persephone…everything Persephone…everything Persephone
everything Persephone…everything Persephone…everything Persephone
everything Persephone…everything Persephone…everything Persephone

    Michael's arms lift upward to the sky as he starts singing along with their enchanted chorus. He dances up and down in the center of the lateral-swaying circle. Out of the black, a large white owl swoops down from a nearby treetop…hooting as it glides down across the slope. Several feet northwest of the circle, the fire's rapidly corroding embers crack loud and clear as the moon sails straight overhead.

7

Time: *8:23 PM, September 7, 1987*
Place: *Room 230, Boulderama Hotel, Boulder COLORADO*

    "The power center inside the solar plexus gets corded when people want your energy or when someone gets you to do for them or…from people needing your approval. Just reverse the procedures for cords leaving you from this area and…don't forget to breathe."

    Gabrielle sits, entranced by his words and the internal experience they now refer to. Her right palm slowly scans her solar plexus until it registers the discordant resonance of foreign energy. Her eyebrows rise involuntarily. She gently pulls out a single, indistinct stream of somebody else's energy. Its elongated dendrite-like endings unravel from the nerve cluster of her solar plexus. Sighing with relief, she sends the cord back to its source… out to the horizontal plane of human interactions.

    "Now, inhale earth energy into the solar plexus and spin it around in there. After the spin cycle, send your own demands for power, feeling and security down to the earth. Send cords from the bottom three centers down into the planet and hook them in. Get a sense of what it feels like to rely on the earth for these three needs. Start sucking up the earth into these centers. When you get around to it, tell me how you feel."

She sits still, breathing steadily for a moment. "I can't believe the difference."

Raphael snaps back. "Then don't. Just experience it." She exhales another sigh of relief. "You got it. When you feel ready to move on, let me know by raising a hand and lowering it." Gabrielle raises her arm effortlessly and lets it drift down onto her lap. "OK, I'm going to brief you on the next three centers…the heart, throat and visionary chakras. The heart governs all forms of love, from romantic to spiritualized…where people want to be their friend, lover, etc. The throat signals your ability to listen and gets corded when someone wants you to hear them out, listen to their pain or how great they are. The visionary center is very simple and subtle. It basically engages our **attention**…where somebody insists that you see them, or where you demand that someone see you. I don't mean mere looking here, but the kind of seeing associated with clairvoyance…as in, **seeing through.** Any questions?"

She adjusts her sitting position. "No. So far, so good."

"Good because I need a cigarette break now, and you need to work without me around. If you're done before I get back, recheck your grounding in all the lower centers." He vigorously rubs his palms together, presses them against his face absorbing their heat. He stands up, stretches, and walks toward the door.

Gabrielle's face turns slightly towards the door. "Raphael?"

He turns halfway around. "Yeah?"
"Thanks."

Half gasping, a brief burst of laughter escapes his mouth. "Thank yourself, man…you've got your work cut out for you." He picks up his black leather jacket hanging by the door and pulls a pack of Russian cigarettes out of its side pocket. Turning around once more before leaving, he faintly whispers:
"You're welcome."

8

Time: *10:33 PM, September 7, 1987*
Place: *A hillside overlooking the Goddess Guild, Malibu*

    Twelve goddesses carry Michael on their shoulders down the hill as Arielle leads them all to the Guild's redwood terrace. There, they place his limp body down on the floorboards, the blond wig partially covering his lipstick-smeared face. The soiled, red velvet dress is in disarray, wrapped tightly around one leg, leaving the other exposed to his thigh. Six women enter the house together and seven remain by his side. Two of these then ignite a tightly-wound bundle of wild sage, blowing its thickening smoke in between the spaces of everybody there. The youngest goddess, Dara, arrives with a silver bowl of water and rose petals. She bends down at Michael's feet and begins washing them very slowly. Michael sighs out loud, deep pleasure and contentment in his now low and resonant voice.
    Arielle moves from his side to sit above him, cradling his head in her long, cold fingers. "Michael…you've done well. The Goddess has accepted you into Her circle. Honor Her in every woman you meet and she will stay with you and you will never be without the feeling you now know in your soul. Goddess has graced you with the return of your very soul and her name is Persephone. This name is also your Goddess mantra." Michael whispers the name. "It will remind you of the Goddess path when you stray. By fulfilling your devotion to Goddess, you are free to become a God. As long as you honor the path that led you here, you shall remain in the Garden. To forget or dishonor this pact, God turns into Devil, and you, Michael, return to your previous ignorance and hatred of women." A shudder involuntarily erupts from his pelvic region, simultaneously rippling up through his head and down to his feet, tipping over the silver bowl…rose petals gliding on the water's surface as it all spills out.

9

Time: *8:35 PM, September 7, 1987*
Place: *Room 230, Boulderama Hotel, Boulder COLORADO*

Raphael opens the door to room 230, quietly slips his cigarettes back into his jacket pocket, and returns to his chair across from Gabrielle. "How's it going?"

She smiles. "Good. I just finished the sixth center as you opened the door."

He flies glances around the room and then rests his gaze a few feet over her left shoulder. "Good timing. Before we go on, I want you to pull neutral cosmic energy from above down through your crown and into the fourth, fifth and sixth centers."

She smiles. "I've already done that. It felt right so I did it as I went along."

He nods his head in approval. "Very good. Do it again, though with a little more focus. Intensify your breath on the inhale…make a laser beam breath. Suck it in and swirl it around in each center on the exhale." Her eyes flutter up into her frontal brain lobes while the corners of her mouth blissfully turn skyward.

"Easy on the trance, Gabriel…there'll be plenty of time for brain change later." She laughs gleefully. "For now, we'll just focus on getting you vertically stable. OK…now we get to find out who owns you. The first cords inside your crown center are going to be from mom and dad. You want to remove these first…gently, with the grace of forgiveness, please."

"I only see one…from my mom."

He looks at the area just over her head. "Looks like dad's fell off some time ago…just like a dead limb."

She reassures herself. "There's no problem with dad. Mom holds me back though. I mean, I can't tell how…or why…it's just a feeling I get when I talk to her on the phone and sometimes… when I just think of her."

He accelerates his psychic trance…eyes fluttering up into his head, the tiny blissful smile, the upraised palm scanning the area over Gabrielle's head. "You've a blind spot around your own authority, Gabrielle. When you refuse to confess your knowledge and area of expertise, you end up having to get caught up in other people's authority trips until you're ready to own your own. Instinctively, you feel that your mother is stronger and wiser than you. Socially, you get along real well, but as animals…you'd like to whoop her ass but good to reclaim lost territory."

Gabrielle breathes deep before gasping. "You see all that?!"

His mouth twists into a sardonic smile. "No, I smell it. Yes, I see it." She withdraws temporarily and then, reproaches him. "What do you mean by 'lost territory'? I kind of get what you mean but…could you spell it out a little more…I'm sorry…"

He laughs. "Relax, you've just lost some turf. Until you confess your authority, it won't make any sense to permit mom's territorial signals. You'll always feel like a little animal around a larger animal, while secretly resenting it. Your resentment holds you back. When your own knowingness governs your life, it'll be easier to permit the autonomy of others…especially your mom's. What's so ironic here is that your crown chakra is rather well-developed while your awareness of it is not. This means you **already know.** Your homework is *knowing that you know.* Somehow, you've been convinced otherwise, and your mom apparently, somehow, reinforces the self-denial in this area."

"Of course, she would. I'm still a little girl to her and that keeps her in charge or, at least, it keeps things familiar enough to keep the ball in her court most of the time."

He nods his head and applauds. "Bravo! Mother's are like that, yeah they are." They both laugh. "As you can see, the problem's not with your mother, but your reluctance to confess knowledge. See how obvious your knowingness around this is? You've known this all along, right? Don't even answer that. Instead, kindly ask your mom to stop sitting on your head and then, pull the cord out…gently." Gabrielle concentrates while reaching her hand above her head. There she grasps the indistinct stream of light and starts pulling.

"What if it doesn't want to come out?"

"If you have to try, just stop. This stuff won't work with effort. We'll have to implement a more serious tactic. Rest your attention deep inside the center of your brain. From here, visualize your mother in front of you on a raised stage. Got it?" She nods. "Now, dress her up in oversized pajamas with little red hens all over it." She nods, smiling. "Now, multiply her by twelve so you see twelve replicas of your mother in oversized pajamas with little red hens all over them. Now, make them all dance the can-can together…you know, all in a row?" Gabrielle's smile widens until it can no longer contain the laughter swelling up inside from her belly.

"Stay with it…as you're laughing, pull the cord out of your crown and send it back to mama." He witnesses her hysterical laughter while she pulls out her mother's psychic influence, releasing it back to its source in the horizontal realm of human interactions. "Now, breathe deep…breathe down the cosmic energy and swirl it around your crown." She breathes with great relief, tears rolling down her cheeks. "When you're ready, send your heart and soul into the eighth center above your head…in space."

Gabrielle breathes deep several times, maintaining the internal concentration she knows she needs to make this work. Gathering her forces into a ball of light inside her brain, she shoots up and out of her head into the suspended center above. Upon contact, she projects her entire being into its transparent heart. **Everything instantly disappears**…noise turns silent…motion stops…and the space…the glorious, infinite space…is *everywhere at once*.

TREMBLE THE GROUND

1

"What are trees?! I tell you they are like your telephones, only better. They keep growing, they help us breathe and they offer themselves freely. Learn to listen to trees and they will let you talk through them."
**GUBOO TED THOMAS, Chief Aboriginal Elder,
Yuin Tribe of Australia**

Time: *Sunrise, February 13, 1988*
Place: *Ayer's Rock, Central Australia*

The sun rises, illuminating the land and the several thousand people who gather at the base of the sacred, ochre-red mountain. Here, whites and aborigines alike prepare together for a sunrise ceremony, collecting wood for the large fire started earlier. Some aboriginal tribal members are climbing the mountain alone. Others remain behind making offerings to Darama, the Great Spirit, through the non-stop buzzing drones of their didgeridoos...their dead, termite-hollowed trees converted into musical instruments.

The white people have arrived from many parts of the world and are, for the most part, dressed in bright festive colors. Many aborigines are dressed in white people's clothes except for those playing didgeridoos and others climbing the mountain. These are nude or half-dressed, painted in the traditional aboriginal x-ray style...skeleton style...bright, white spots and streaks...across dark, moving bodies.

The metallic humming of didgeridoos and the click-clack clapping of clapsticks infuse the air with the trance of the aboriginal dreamtime. Everyone here is busy learning their place. The whites are learning the ways of the aborigine. The aboriginals are learning the law of the mountain. The mountain is absorbing the interstellar beam of galactic information now arriving direct from the galaxy's core at twenty-seven degrees Sagittarius. Deep inside the red mountain's cool, hollow heart, a large electric-blue crystal receives and refracts this cosmic signal…radiating it out to the aboriginal people climbing its skin…who, in turn, move the trembling light around the planet's surface.

Meanwhile, back at the foot of Ayer's Rock, thousands of whites and blacks gather around to hear the invocation of a chief aboriginal elder. "This is the working of the ceremony to save the green ants, the aboriginal people and the dreamtime that holds the world together. The white people are too young to know this and too old to understand. Yet, you must listen to these words now and hear with your hearts, the singing of the mountain. **The mountain sings.** It sings like it has never sung before…it is singing now for you…for us…for every living creature on this beautiful earth. The mountain sings its first and last song. The music comes from far, far away yet it is inside you…inside the mountain…inside the trees…inside the rising sun…inside the stars…inside the little pebbles in the river…inside the kangaroo…inside the green ants…inside your mother…inside your father…the song is singing by itself inside every living thing. Now, the mountain sings to keep the world alive. When you hear the song inside your hearts, sing back to the mountain. Sing back to the mountain… **sing back to the mountain…**"

To the backdrop soundtrack of a hundred didgeridoos and clapsticks, thousands of people sound a rainbow chorus of tones, chants and melodies…cadencing into an aural patchwork of multitudinous, wordless song.

2

Time: *The Great Collapse*
Place: *PSI-Bank Memory Matrix, Planetary Limbic System*

I do my best work at the darkest hour before dawn, after all the nonsense and before the human survival machine awakens each morning shift. It's really the only decent time to let go…burp, fart, exfoliate and vomit, if I have to. There are poisonous gases inside me just dying to breakthrough this surface tension of horizontal human noise. *This is why earthquakes and eruptions are so profoundly satisfying at this hour.* While we're at it, maybe you can do something about all those hideous underground nuclear tests?! They're giving me the worst case of hemorrhaging imaginable... Good thing I'm spinning too fast to stop and bleed to death.

When enough humans realize the ritual application of Spin, perhaps you'll find something more creative to do than bugger me with all those obsolete oil rigs. Then again, perhaps, you won't...my sighs are hurricanes, my sneezes...avalanches...and when I shrug my shoulders, some people are going to fly...

Not to change the subject, but maybe you could also ease up on all that uranium mining? How do you expect my natives to keep doing their magic without all that precious, underground hoppy action?! That doubles for our six-legged interstellar ambassadors, the giant dreaming green ants of Australia. Once they die, sayonara Mr. &Mrs. Human Being. Oh, one last thing. Whoever's walking off with my crystallizations, better chill out. You know who you are. Bury those crystals you're hoarding if you know what's good for us. Bury them under my skin. Bury them in hexagonal formations and all will be forgiven. Do this wherever my ravines, trees and rivers converge. Then, stand over the natural meeting points of my splendorous curves and I'll shoot a warm, wavy thrill up your hungry coccyx.

3

Time: *6:29 PM, October 11, 1987*
Place: *An office building in Marina Del Rey, CALIFORNIA*

Inside behind the red-brick tinted glass office front, a tired receptionist sits reading the classified section of Los Angeles' most popular New Age magazine. Her diffused attention scans the personals ads, half-searching for dreams while the other half works overtime to stay awake. Arielle walks in through the front door, hot and bright as an angel in heat. The receptionist continues scrying the magazine for her future, while waving her right hand up in the air like an S.O.S. signal on the high seas. "Hi, Ari...how long you staying tonight?"

Arielle waves back. "Part-time...and you?"

She peeks at her briefly, then returns her gaze to the search. "I've been here since four in the morning."

She checks the bulletin board by the door for messages. "You look it..."

The receptionist stops reading and looks blankly at the mess of words swimming before her delirious mind. "How can you tell? You can't even see me."

Arielle crosses the room, peers over the magazine and down onto her haggard yet fragile face...her sea green eyes swimming dizzily in her head. "Yup...you look it. Get some sleep, dearest." She walks away and enters an open archway leading down a corridor of multi-colored, numbered doors.

"Hey, Ari...what's a 'Harmonic Convergence'?"

Arielle laughs as she searches her purse for a key. "Something you'll *never* have to worry about. Just think of it as...the **Harmonica Virgins...**"

The receptionist's laugh is interrupted by a smoker's cough. "Harmonica virgins! You mean there's still something untouched inside of me?!" She continues laughing and coughing.

"Untouched, unopened and undone..." The purple door swings open as she walks into the cubicle of a room. Much like the dozen other cubicles behind each colored door, it is equipped with a beanbag chair, telephone and whatever each employee brings to kill dead time. She turns on the soft overhead light, drops her purse to the floor and turns the switch on the red telephone to the "on" position. Sitting down, she begins reviewing the pages torn from the pornographic pulp novels she taped onto the wall earlier. The top of each page is marked in large red letters, categorizing its individual fetish: BJ, DOMINANT, SUBMISSIVE, TEASE, S&M, STRAIGHT, BI, BONDAGE and KINKY.

The phone rings. She takes a deep breath, exhales and answers it in her breathiest, most emotional voice. "Hello...what can we do for you?" After a silence, the raspy panting of heavy breathing reverberates inside her receiver. "Oh, honey...I wish I was there to help you out. What's your name, sweetheart?" Suddenly, the heavy breathing bursts wide open into hellacious laughter. Her face flushes white and then, pink.

A familiar male voice gasps out. "Arielle...I just had to call you." Arielle sits upright. "Who?! No, this is Kathy... I'm sorry, I think you've got the wrong number...but maybe I can help you out, honey..."

"Arielle! It's me, Michael. I'm sorry for calling you here like this but..."

Her face reddens with rage. "Michael, what on Earth!?"

She catches her breath, resorting to calm. "Who told you? Dara? It was Dara, wasn't it? Well now...what can I possibly do for you?!"

"I'm in love with you, Arielle. I can't stop thinking about...that night we spent together, I mean, the whole thing...the ritual, the goddesses...everything... I'm an absolute wreck..."

She smiles warily. "Oh, Michael...that's sweet but I just can't accept your anima projections. Remember what we agreed to... keeping our noses clean, remember?"

He sighs into the mouthpiece. "I feel torn apart, like I've been left inside...a non-stop rinse cycle..."

She touches two fingers to her lips, as if to remind herself. "You're still processing the ceremony, aren't you? Well, let's get you inside a cool, dry spin cycle then..." They both laugh uneasily. "Don't you know you're dealing with the full-gale force of Persephone? It's got to be tough going at first."

Michael's exhale reverberates inside her receiver. "What do you expect me to do? I mean I'm willing to work through this, but I don't have a clue as to what to do. I feel like a zombie. I could use a little help, y'know..."

She softens her voice. "Do you know this call is costing you a dollar a minute?"

Another exhale pushes its way into his mouthpiece. "Yes, I know. I figured it was the only way to reach you. Since you said it was best we didn't see each other... I don't mind. It's worth the information, Ari."

She ponders his intention for a moment. "That's rather chivalrous in a way…and I like that. So, let's start from the beginning then. Tell me what you're feeling. What's actually happening inside you?" Michael inhales twice, struggling with his words. "Just blurt it out, Michael."

"I love you and there's this damn fire in my chest and it's got your name on it, OK?! That's it. I think I'm in love…in fact, I'm sure I am. No doubt about it, I'm in love with you Arielle and I can't stop thinking about you. I can't get you out of my mind. There…that's it…"

Shaking her head, she mutters to herself. "Falling in love can be so dogmatic."

She takes one deep breath. "Listen. This is a classic occupational hazard of Goddess work. Listen again: you've confused your anima with me. I claim responsibility for having initiated you to Her, and now it's up to you to embrace Her. She is alive, burning inside of **you.** You've just confused the message with the messenger by…tacking my face onto the force of your own soul. If your ego keeps dogmatically **insisting** that I'm *it*…your soul… you'll keep spinning your wheels inside the parking lot of Chapel Perilous."

A silence momentarily cools Michael. "Chapel Perilous?"

Arielle takes another deep breath. "You're a fatal romantic, Michael, waiting in line to be heartbroken and you're about to be disillusioned." Michael's voice explodes. "That's just great! Here I am practically down on my knees confessing absolute, unconditional love for you, and you tell me I'm about to attend my execution. You know…you are one cold, cruel lady…Arielle."

She waits a few moments before speaking. "There's nothing unconditional about your love, and you're mistaking your disappointment with feelings of persecution. I've nothing to defend, Michael so…I won't be fighting you. I've seen these symptoms before and I'll probably see them again; however, as long as you insist on blaming me for your pain, you'll remain in Chapel Perilous."

Michael's thinking returns for the first time in the conversation. "Chapel Perilous...what is this place you keep talking about? What are you talking about?"

Jubilant, Arielle applauds. "Bravo, bravo! Bellissima! You're listening. That's progress."

Michael accepts his fate with a sigh of relief. "OK...you're right. I've been on non-stop ego since I called. I feel so helpless though."

She sighs with relief while sitting back in her cushioned chair. "Now you're talking. Those feelings of helplessness are real, Michael, and there's no way of ignoring them. You are up against an extremely powerful force in your psyche and until you come to terms with Her, you'll keep feeling them. In fact, every time you lose touch with Her like this, you'll feel more helpless than ever."

Michael's bewilderment infuses the silence. "You mean it's OK to feel helpless?"

Her buoyant laugh catches him off guard. "Of course, silly. What else can you do when you're feeling helpless than to just feel helpless? **Feeling** helpless doesn't mean you **are** helpless, although sometimes I wonder about you men. To get out of Chapel Perilous learn to become **as still as death.** Then you may be able to slip out unnoticed and maybe even exit with your silliest mind intact."

Michael questions her. "As still as death. You mean, meditate?"

"If that helps. You see, Michael...you're inflamed right now. You need to...chill out...lighten up...OK?" Her joyous giggles burst forth. "If you get out of the Chapel alive, there are some things you're going to have do to restabilize your shape...your, uh, american male ego."

Michael's exasperated sigh swims into the mouthpiece. "How do you know all these things?! Where does all this stuff come from?!"

Her voice is matter-of-fact. "Goddess Training. Something you'll never have to concern yourself with in this lifetime. Yet, since we've met, I'm obliged to share what's appropriate to our predicament."

Michael's voice resigns itself. "What is appropriate?"

She thinks inside their shared silence. "It seems you're much more of an intellectual than a moralist in the long run, so your path to the heart is ushered by Dr. Death." Michael's soft gasp warns her of his anxiety. "Oh, don't be such a corny literalist, Michael. Dr. Death just wants to make sure you know how to still yourself."

"As in...being as still as death?"

"As still as a death. **IF** you get out alive...and that's entirely up to you...and how dead still you can be, but if you find the exit, there are certain Goddess tasks you must do to reassemble that poor broken ego of yours. That way you won't have to depend on me to mother you back to life."

Another silence enters Michael. "Thanks...I guess that would help. Arielle...I feel so...formless...I feel like I need a handle...some definite thing to do or, I'm going to make a royal mess of myself."

She laughs and sighs. "Listen. Just because a woman has the power to undo you and leave you a naked mess, it doesn't mean she's responsible for sheltering you afterwards. It's up to the man to rearrange himself after he annihilates himself in the liquid skies of true love."

4

Time: *The Great Collapse*
Place: *PSI-Bank Memory Matrix, Planetary Neo-Cortex*

If you're going to do something right, you've got to do it yourself. Unless, of course, there's cooperation from activated participants who are ready, willing and able to share the power. It seems the second alternative is a far more intelligent course of action, and since **action is real**, *arrangements have been made. Our special forces are now circulating amidst your surface tension, seeking fusion with the human conduits currently preparing for* **mutual acceleration.** *As usual, all awakening emanations will bypass the cocoons of human ignorance...*

insulating their black, sleeping butterflies from catastrophic, premature arousal, that is, with the exception of **leaks,** *or humans miracles. Otherwise, we shall proceed with business as usual. There's a planet to feed, a star to seed, and a Supreme Being to attend to…*

5

Time: *3:33 PM, October 20, 1987*
Place: *The SATURN CAFE in Boulder, Colorado*

Cigarette smoke spirals aimlessly above and behind the TEDs' heads. All seven crouch languidly around a large table at the back of the room. Raphael looks around and then, momentarily, at each of them. As he lights his second cigarette, a waiter attempts to bus their table. Only Raphael's eyes move to meet the waiters' as he issues a definite but clearly courteous command.

"Not done yet."

The waiter instantly recoils his grasp and lunges for the next table. Raphael looks at Savitri, the only woman in the TED… the only woman, he thought, disillusioned enough to tolerate the self-exposure of the great work. She returns his gaze. He takes in the pervasive heat of her dark, smoldering eyes…a black fire burning behind a glacial facade of broken, Victorian beauty. Both nod together in the silent recognition of secrets shared and pacts kept over the past four years.

He sucks his cigarette, blowing the smoke upwards to the ceiling. "This dead zone isn't going to last forever. Thanks to Wall Street, people are now more aware than ever of the collapse. I figure we've got until mid-February of next year to open the gate. By the way, the upcoming Saturn-Uranus conjunction last occurred in 1942, during the blackest hole of World War II. By February 17th next year, with the Chinese Year of the Dragon, the Zeitgeist of '88 should be well underway. Until then, I'm calling off our mobile temple construction unit. That type of temple construction has been, for the most part, easy prey. Too easy. Quite frankly, I'm bored with it. Besides, I've gotten the good word from Cardinal Hyatt of the Gnostic Catholic Church that portable altars aren't cutting it these days. On top of that, if we don't stabilize our own temple soon, we'll be plagued by an epidemic of bad timing. Comments?" He nonchalantly glances around.

Everyone except Savitri is either shaking their heads or looking away.

She gazes down into her cup of swirling tea leaves, opening her mouth in disbelief. "You actually told him what we were doing?"

Raphael smiles, sipping his creamed iced coffee and laughs. "Are you kidding?! He'd probably excommunicate me on the spot. No, I just told him we were temporarily experimenting with portable temples and rotating altars. He said it was way too advanced. So, I guess that means we settle down and get married…"

Savitri looks up in mock surprise. "Oh, Ricky! Does this mean we get to dress up and really play house instead of staying at all those crummy motels along the way?"

Raphael laughs for the second time. "That's the idea. We pool our resources, rent a place and set up a real live temple. It'd have to be a place far enough away from downtown to not attract outsiders. The good Cardinal Hyatt is preparing me for the inner order rituals, and so I will consider presenting initiation to the lesser levels for those interested. And since we're going to be playing inside the law now, I'd like to change the name of our temple and even open it up to neophytes. Any suggestions?"

Savitri sips her Darjeeling tea, watching the rest of them restlessly thinking. She selects her moment carefully, a split-second lapse of silence in between their grinding thoughts. "I propose we invite the Goddess back in. I really do believe it's time. Consecrate the temple with devic spirits…goddess knows there's plenty of them around here…and then, invoke the name of **Isis**."

Raphael nods passionately. "That's precisely what I've had in mind. We can start the polarization prep rites now and cultivate the garden space for Horus."

A TED member laughs. "It is bloody obvious, isn't it?" Every other group member nods, grunts and otherwise motions their instantaneous unanimous approval.

Savitri looks upwards, clasping her hands. "We'll need another priestess for this to work. Someone new. Somebody who's already pretty psychic, but hasn't fallen into the trappings yet… someone fresh, someone unjaded." Raphael's eyes shift towards her, then towards the cafe entrance where Gabrielle and Suzanne suddenly appear. He looks back to her and then, to the two women standing in the coffee line. "Vitch vun, commandant?" Raphael's eyes are glued to the entrance, watching how each woman adjusts to the inevitable, yet subtle, psychic shock of entering the Saturn Cafe. "Which one do you think, Lucy?"

Savitri scans their shrinking and expanding auras and without looking back at him, speaks while assessing their energetic intentions. "They've got this symbiotic thing going, don't they? They're like two ends of a single battery, one's a plus and the other's the minus. Why, there's practically a whole woman between them." She laughs at her comment. "I think the receptive one's our girl."

He shakes his head. "I think not. Look to see."

She closes her eyes, fluttering them briefly back up into her head. A small rapturous smile bends the corners of her mouth upward as she softly chuckles. "How right you are, Ricky. She's a whole lot stronger than she lets on. She is priestess material, isn't she?" He nods. "The other one? Now I see what you were getting at. She's a natural! A beautiful, wide-eyed natural all stressed out with nowhere to go."

She opens her eyes. The cafe lights twinkle off the thin film of opaque coating on her pupils. "Ahhh, I needed that. Nothing like a mid-afternoon pick-me-up trance…"

"Lucy, how about we make pretend we didn't see anything. They'll no doubt run into us and, if they do, I'll introduce you." They both simultaneously raise their cups in a toast. "Here's to

Isis and Her future temple. May the right place come to us so we may serve Her every whim, desire and extraordinary…"

Savitri's eyes illumine from the inside. "Passion."

Raphael continues the toast. "Here's to Her extraordinary passion." As they all raise their mugs for a final toast, Gabrielle and Suzanne casually stroll by…holding trays of iced water, cappuccinos and fluffy, French pastries. Raphael raises his cup into the air for the third time…this time, directly towards Suzanne. "To Her extraordinary passion."

Suzanne blushes, smiles wildly and stumbles after Gabrielle across the room four tables away. She leans over Gabrielle's shoulder, gasping. 'What do you think he meant by that?"

They both set their trays down onto the table. "Looked like a pass to me, Suzy." Suzanne mechanically sits down, picks up her cappuccino and, sips long hard gulps. "So what'd he tell you in your reading? How was it?"

Gabrielle ponders her enormous question. "It was quite extraordinary. He ran me through some trancework and psychic clearing. I opened up places inside me that have never been opened before."

Suzanne's impatience jumps again. "But…what did he tell you?"

Gabrielle brushes her bangs aside with her left hand and sips her cappuccino with her right. "He said I was as dead as a Tibetan doornail. He just kept hitting it with a hammer is what he did. I had no idea what a dead zone I've been in…that I'm still in."

Gabrielle bites down into the sweet, flaky pastry. "He seemed to know a lot about death…how deadness works…what it's used for. The guy's utterly on the mark, Suzy." Her face contracts into a big frozen smile. "Oh, you don't have to worry…he's not my type. Fascinating to death, but definitely not my type. Well, speak of the devil."

Suzanne turns her head and there, standing a bit too tall, are Raphael and Savitri. Raphael raises his sunglasses off his eyes to rest on his forehead. "Hi Gabrielle…how's it going today?"

She looks up and meets his strangely muted gaze. "So far, so good. How about you?"

He silently nods his head, mugging mock smugness. "Not too shabby. Howdy Suzanne. I'd like to introduce you to a very good friend of mine whose activities may possibly interest you. Suzanne, meet Savitri."

The two women simultaneously ease into each other's presence. Savitri extends both hands towards her. "Nice to meet you, Suzanne."

Suzanne's perpetual hedonic smile reaches through her hands. "Nice to meet you, too, Savitri. What kind of activities is Raphael talking about?"

Savitri smiles warmly, her dark moon-like eyes reflecting back her obvious appreciation and enthusiasm. "Goddess rituals."

Suzanne's eyes widen with intrigue and intense magnetic fascination. "Goddess rituals?! I'd like to talk to you about some dreams I've had…"

Savitri nods. Her eyes assure her of complete unwavering attention as her lips form easily into a perfect, cryptic smile.

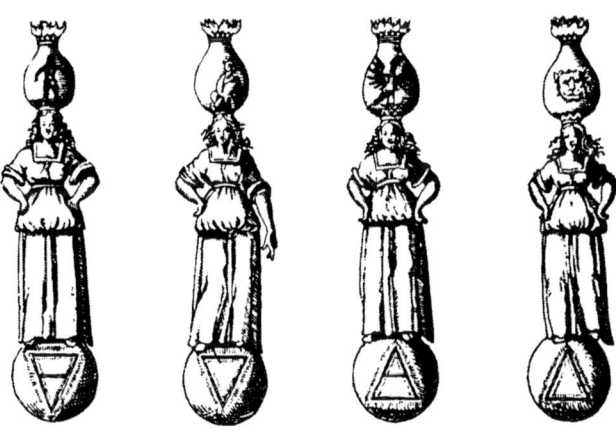

6

Time: *7:07 PM, October 11, 1987*
Place: *On the telephone, an office building in Marina Del Rey, CA*

Arielle reassures Michael. "I believe in you, so here's what I suggest. Until you figure out how to begin putting the pieces of your puzzled self back again, devote three different levels of activity to Persephone: physically, emotionally, and mentally. Find three simple tasks, like…run a mile every day **just for Her. Sing to Her** every morning in the shower. Write a poem every night before you go to sleep and **dedicate it to Her.** Now, it's important that you do this entirely in your own way. Just make sure you do it on all three levels."

Michael exhales in great relief. "That does help. I can't explain what I've been through. It's like I've been walking around like the walking dead…without a soul…like a zombie…an empty shell…totally vacant, gone, Arielle, just gone."

"I've got news for you, Michael."
The silence, again. "Yeah?"
"You **are** a zombie…a pathetic, empty shell of a man. Everything you are experiencing now is quite real. In fact, your real life has just begun."
"Everything I experience is real. My real life has just begun. Great. Can I ask you one last question?"
"Ask away, Michael."
He hesitates. "Why do you do this…how come? I mean…this work…"

Her laugh flutters into the air. "Phone sex?" She laughs again. "It's Goddess work. It's good business. Sometimes, it's even fun. In that order. With the AIDS epidemic on the loose, lots of men turn to phone sex. Some call just to talk…others tell me their problems and feel so relieved to be listened to by a woman that they never get around to the sex part. I have to admit, most of them do call for sex. It's a unique service, really."

Michael's voice sours in disdain. "The world's oldest profession?"

"Look at it this way, Mikey. Just consider us modern-day, electronic tele-courtesans. I mean, most of the girls here don't have this kind of perspective so they're in it for the money and, sometimes, the sheer power of it. I never thought of it before, Michael, but it's also a genuine outlet for my...compassion."

"I believe it." Michael inhales. "I guess seeing you is out of the question?"

She informs him. "It's not even an option at this stage."

"Then, I guess this is...good-bye, forever?"

"Not so fast, Mr. Dramatic Guy. According to the quantum mechanics of Bell's Theorem, any two particles once in actual contact will continue to influence each other no matter how far apart in time and space they may subsequently move. We've been in actual contact, Michael. In other words, you can run but you can't hide. We'll see us in the future."

He laughs then, sighs. "You're too much. No, you are simply way cool. Thanks, Arielle...thanks for everything..."

She laughs lightly. "Here's...to the future?"

He joins her. "To the future..." They tread the ensuing silence with nothing to say, and then Arielle hangs up her line. The vacant dial tone passes through Michael's ears and into his busy brain.

MAGNETIC ARRANGEMENTS

1

"The less something exists, the more people want it."
ee cummings, from his one-act play, SANTA CLAUS

Time: *Sunrise, November 1, 1987*
Place: *The kitchen in Michael's apartment, San Fernando Valley, Los Angeles,* **CALIFORNIA**

Michael writes furiously...occasionally looking up, past the streams of sunlight shooting across the kitchen. He attacks the paper again, scrawling word after word, nanoseconds after they appear on the screen of his inflamed mind. In a final abrupt gesture, he throws his pen across the room where it breaks against the wall. "There! I am without a doubt, forever gone and deliriously yours..." Picking the paper up, he gazes into it like a window and reads his poem out loud.

A Man greets his Death
Bringing the Woman to Life
When his fleeting, fickle attention
Stops. Settles...in the warmth of Her Womb...

While dissolving the crystal of his Pride
A Man fights for his Sanity
Bringing the Woman to Life,
A Man fights for his Life.

When a Man disappears into the Woman
His precious Vision consumed by Her Soul,
He awaits the Time She returns to Him
The Gift of Love...Restored & Refined.

Then a Real Man directs this Love
Onto His Mechanical Apparatus
And...in the Splendourous Awakening
Asks the Woman to Dance.

2

Time: *3:21 PM, November 1, 1987*
Place: *Backyard, Gabrielle's and Adam's House, Boulder CO*

Gabrielle lay facedown on the ground, sobbing into the dark green grass...her hands clutching the blackened topsoil, squeezing tight its tiny rounded pebbles and whitened roots. Several mosquitoes buzz and bounce nimbly into the air above her trembling body. Inside a heavy sigh, she sinks deeper into the grass...her senses opening to the soft, magnetic waves passing through her from below. Subtle pulses of planetary emanation make their way into the widening cracks of her collapsing defenses, gently massaging the undulating aetheric double of her now...motionless...body.

Her head...slowly...turns to the side. The Earth's numinous emanation pushes through her tear-flooded, opening eyes...shining forth from the dead stillness of her body. Involuntarily, her body inhales, embraces the ground and then, lets go...sinking deeper into the Earth. Breathing in its massive vitality, Gabrielle surrenders her grip. The tension holding her entire life together now melts into the living planetary entity. Simultaneously, the Earth absorbs her broken will into itself while rearranging its pieces to align with their deepening mutual resonance. A burning calm expands inside her heart, opening a vast inner gratitude.

Adam enters through the front doorway of the house toting sacks of groceries and calling Gabrielle's name. He walks into the kitchen, places the bags on the table and mechanically checks the Answering Machine for incoming messages. Finding none, he looks blankly out the window into the backyard. Automatically, his eyes focus in on Gabrielle's motionless body. His body jerks as he turns and runs for the backdoor, lunging into the backyard...stopping abruptly in front of her. He takes a deep breath while his eyes instantly scan for signs of life. "Gabrielle? Are you alright?" Gabrielle grunts. He sighs an awkward laugh of relief to himself. "OK. Grunt once for yes, two for no and three for

NO COMMENT, GO AWAY, I'M HAVING A GOOD TIME." Gabrielle grunts thrice and they both start shaking with laughter. Turning around to face him, her eyes squint in the afternoon sunlight. "Adam, I love you. You're so…civilized."

3

Time: *The Great Collapse*
Place: *EXTRATERRESTRIAL OUT-REACH PROGRAM, Earth's Core*

It seems to Us that your human civilization is now feeding almost entirely on its acquired horizontal stability again. We are losing contact with reciprocal sustenance at this time and request your assistance. They have successfully poured their essences into an irrevocable, horizontal feeding frenzy, and as such, have completely forgotten their originating vertical source. This widespread spillage of vital essences has reached the critical density necessary for Us to contact you. The vast majority of humans have already made their conversion into the potency food to nurture the next phase of your evolution as their Creators. Mothers and Fathers of the Future, the fruit is falling and the ground is ripe. Return to Earth and reap your harvest.

ALERT: *There will be survivors of great innocence that shall be spared and not eaten. These are Our future children. They have turned to Us for sustenance. They have restored their vertical stability by certain horizontal sacrifices and will remain intact in their cocoons until ready to blossom. These baby gods are incubating in the womb of Our omni-directional love. By giving their bodies to Us, their horizontal investment is disconnect and their integrity conduits realigned with planetary intention. The Earth current speaks through their souls to other children they meet along the way, and this is how they find each other during their Great Collapse. The rest are yours…*

4

Time: *Sunset, November 1, 1987*
Place: *Kitchen, Gabrielle and Adam's House, Boulder, CO*

      Gabrielle sits at the wooden kitchen table, peeling an orange…thinking about how she will express her thoughts to Adam who is unpacking the groceries into the refrigerator and adjoining cabinets. She watches him from the corner of her eye, cocking her head slightly to change the angle of her vision. "Adam? I'm leaving Boulder for awhile…maybe a few days… maybe a few weeks or months, I don't know yet. I just need to travel and get away…"
      He continues unpacking vegetables and neatly arranging them in the bottom plastic drawer of the refrigerator. "When?" She nibbles at her bright, sour orange peel. "Soon, like, maybe tomorrow." She watches him closely for his reactions.
  He stops and turns to her, looking at her with a calm she had not seen before. "Do you need a ride to the airport?"
  Caught off-guard, she looks away. "No. I'm not flying. I'd like to drive, but I don't feel safe taking my car and was wondering if you would consider trading me for the jeep until I return."

He thinks to himself, momentarily suspended by her request. "I think that can be arranged. I'm not going out of state for at least another six months or so."

She reassures him. "Oh, I'll be back way before then. You must know something, Adam. The changes I'm going through are definitely internal. You are not the problem. You are, if anything... totally understanding, to a fault perhaps. And, so don't blame yourself for my...state...my distance. I mean, I'm not asking you to stay cool about it, either. I just need to let go of everything right now...everything." She stops and wonders. "Aren't you just a little bit pissed?!"

Adam's right hand tenses around the bottle of organic apple juice. He jumps up and hurls it against the kitchen wall where it shatters, shooting liquid apples and slivers of glass everywhere. "Yes, I'm pissed! What do you think?! I thought I was OK with all this...all of your goddam changes!! I thought I'd love you enough to let you go...you know, do the appropriate New Age Course In Miracles kind of thing but...I just can't! I can't!!! Yes...I'm pissed at you for changing on me like this! Who wouldn't be?"

Trembling with rage, he stands looking at her...searching for her response...yearning to see where she really stood with him now.

Gabrielle places the orange down on the table while looking at it "I'm glad. You're right. You've got every right to feel this way and...I don't have anything to say except that I'm sorry that I've hurt you. I'm sorry, Adam."

Adam watches her focus on the orange. "Yeah, I'm sorry, too. I'm sorry it didn't turn out the way we had planned it from the start. I'm sorry we were broken into. I'm sorry we never got to get married. I'm sorry we never got to have children."

She looks at him. "I'm not going away forever. I just need some more time and space alone...apart."

He laughs sharply. "More time...more space? You're already gone, Gabrielle...long gone."

5

Time: *Later that night*
Place: *The New Temple of ISIS...the outskirts of North Boulder, CO*

Raphael and Suzanne stand outside the abandoned farmhouse granary the TED had recently leased for their New Temple of Isis. They both speak and smoke cigarettes, Raphael smoking more and talking less. Both are dressed in black. Raphael leans on a cast iron railing, blocking the doorway to the temple. His steel-grey eyes rest calm on her face, absorbing the details of her every reaction. She looks away from his gaze several times, and each time he looks away with her.

He opens his mouth for a moment, then closes it before speaking. "You'll need a magickal name to get inside."

She looks back at him. "What would you suggest?"

Half-surprised, he laughs. "What would *you* suggest?! Nobody can give you a magickal name in this temple except yourself. And you can't get in without one."

Eyes alight, her head bobs gently up and down. "Shekinah... Shekinah is my magickal name."

He nods his head, ever so slightly, in approval. "The feminine angelic force of divine love...appropriate enough. Consider myself a witness. I'd suggest you don't tell anyone else this name until the moment of your initiation...when the Priestess asks you to. Until then, you may wish to enter deep contemplation with it. I presume this name was given to you by your Guardian Angel?" She restrains her surprise and just nods. "Good. You may wish to summon him to go through with you. Any more questions or... uh, answers?"

She laughs, he smiles and they embrace...her head resting on his shoulder. "This feels so natural to me, Raphael. I feel like I've already done this before somewhere."

He gently nudges them apart while rolling his focus onto a spot just above the point between her eyes. "Perhaps you have, Suzanne...perhaps you have. Now, before we enter the temple, I'd like you to place your attention in the middle of your brain. Do this with your eyes open or closed, as you like. But don't try. Just sit and rest in this center. Let this place in the center of your brain be like a soft, large pillow. Allow your awareness to settle into its comfort. This is your psychic command post. From here, pay attention to any changes in your perception and/or your overall state of being. When you start feeling a cool tingling sensation there, say...'*when*'."

Raphael closes his eyes, connecting his complete attention inside his internal vertical sources...above, in the Cosmic Energy of the stars, and below with the Earth Energy of the planet. Instantaneously, a soft blue stream of light passes out his closed eyes, touching her brow and passing into her central brain area. This light finds its target in her pineal gland, bathing it in its pale blue illumination. Then, an intermittent series of tiny ultraviolet sparks traverse through the blue beam...entering her pineal gland, stirring it to wiggle. This cone-shaped gland in the center of her brain slowly oozes the neuro-transmitter chemical, serotonin...sending the cool, tingling sensations of clarity to Suzanne's surface consciousness. The corners of her mouth turn upwards in a small blissful smile. "When, Raphael, when..."

Almost imperceptibly Raphael shakes his head. "Not now, Shekinah, not now. You're not quite ready tonight. Come back in four nights when the moon is full in a long, white dress. Then, you'll be ready." He turns and walks inside the front door to the farmhouse granary, leaving Suzanne behind...smiling with her eyes closed.

6

Time: *The Great Collapse*
Place: *Dept. of EARTH SURRENDER RITES, Atlantean Archives*

Groups of three, six, nine, twelve and thirteen are required to activate reciprocal collective engagement with the planetary entity. The three-fold intention of Earth Surrender Rites are: 1) stabilization of a group mind 2) the connection of a stable group mind with its vertical source of vitality in the Earth and the Stars and... 3) to instruct a vertically-connected, stable group mind towards the balancing of Earth energies oscillating between the planet's core and its surface. The third intention is realized by the virtue of the previous two states requiring absolute human surrender to the Earth. It is the planetary entity that instructs a group mind in the task of intermediating its core and surface forces towards optimum geomantic alignment.

By engaging vertical stability, a group mind may effectively bypass the horizontal and social tendency to feed off each other's personal vitality. Instead, a true group unity may emerge from each individual's total commitment to their own internal spiritual sources and the expression of this integrity outwardly as a state of offering. A mutual autonomy develops with each individual's transmission of Being which, in turn, accelerates the group mind's lowest common denominator of Intelligence. Everything that rises must converge...

7

Time: *8:23 AM, November 2, 1987*
Place: *Michael's apartment, San Fernando Valley, L.A. CA*

Michael kneels...stuffing socks, underwear and t-shirts into an army-green duffel bag. He then gets up and paces around the apartment, looking to see if there's anything else he needs to pack. Stopping abruptly, he turns and runs to the cassette-tape deck in the living room and starts piling cassette tapes into his arms, just as the phone rings. He turns suddenly and all the tapes tumble to the floor. The phone rings again. "Merde! O Man O God O Man O God...I'm coming already!"

He picks up the receiver, drops it to the floor and picks it up again. "Michael here. Jeremiah! Holy cow! Long time, no hear. When was it? Good lord, yeah...so, where are you now? Boulder!? You're not going to believe this...no, you'll believe it alright. Just as you called I was packing my bags for Boulder! I mean...is this the No Coincidences Dept. or what?! What? Why Boulder? I know that Jose Arguelles lives there and I want to see if I can talk with him about the Harmonic Convergence, the Mayan Calendars and basically, you know, what's going down now that the Earth shifts are happening. Do you know Jose? Do you think there's a chance of me meeting him? Uh huh...yeah, he has gotten pretty famous, well, if I'm supposed to, I will. So, what's Boulder really like? Uh huh...is it really this spiritual mecca everybody says it is? A supermarket? Ha! I guess that's unavoidable. There's really a lot going on there, huh? What? Speak up, Jeremiah...I can't hear you very well. Can you speak up? I can barely hear you. Our connection is fading out. Jeremiah? Jeremiah? Are you there?"

Michael rolls his eyes upward to the ceiling, then laughs as he blows a fast, hard breath into the receiver. He puts his ear to the phone again and listens to the constant drone of the familiar dial tone. "O Man O God O Man O God O Man O God…"

8

Time: *8:32 AM, November 2, 1987*
Place: *A gas station, 12 miles north of Boulder in Lyons CO*

Gabrielle is seen talking on the grey telephone inside the gas station phone booth. The service attendants, two middle-aged men in greasy overalls, are shaking their heads and joking at the display of steam and clanking noises spewing forth from her jeep's overheating engine Gabrielle watches the men laugh, her face twisting into a grimace of dread.

"So, Adam…it doesn't look like I'm getting out of Boulder, for awhile anyways. What am I going to do? I think I'll stay with Suzanne for a few days to figure things out. This is rather strange but it feels like…I don't know, like maybe something is making sure I don't leave Boulder right now and…I'm going to stick around to find out what's going on. The jeep? Uh huh…I'll just call Triple-A and have it towed back to the house, if that's OK by you. Uh huh…I'm sorry…real sorry. I can charge it to my Visa card, OK? No, really… I was driving it when it happened. No, I won't have it any other way. No, Adam…absolutely not. OK…OK…OK…if you really have to, we'll split the bill."

One of the gas station attendants walks toward her and stands outside the phone booth, beckoning to her with his right hand. "Hold on, Adam." She slides the folding door open. "Yes?"

"Don't mean to bother you but…you vehicle isn't going anywhere today. Do you want it towed somewheres?"

"After this call, I'm phoning Triple-A to do it. Thanks for the evaluation though. Can you tell what's wrong with it?"

He looks out over the surrounding mountains. "About five-hundred dollars…by the sounds of it, your heads are blown."

She covers the mouthpiece of the receiver. "Five-hundred dollars!?"

He looks back from the mountains to her. "Uh, yup. That's if you do it here. If you bring it into the dealer back there in Boulder, it'll run you almost twice that amount. Maybe more…"

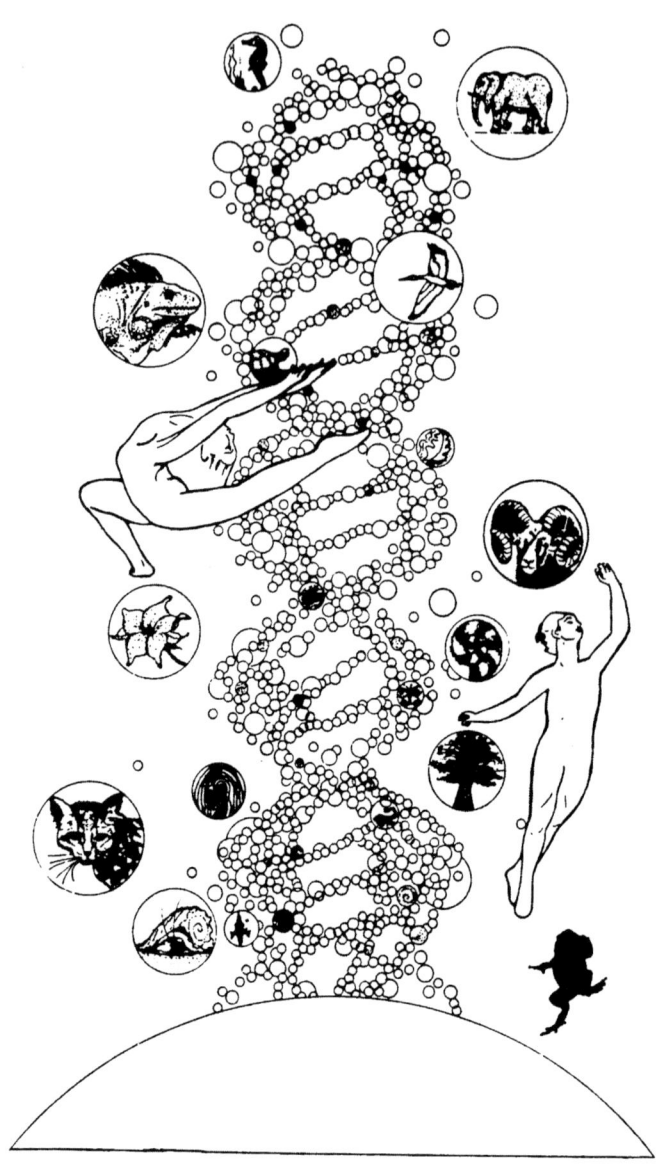

WAVE-FORM SURFING

1

"Think big or stay home."
Ms. BERNIE, Boulder Corporate Executive

Time: *The Great Collapse*
Place: *Council of ASCENDED MASTERS, The Akashic Mansion*

The unbroken chain of ASCENDED MASTERS have, over ages past, offered spiritual guidance to those preparing for a life of service to the Hierarchy of Saints, Angels and Alien Space Beings. In exchange, these human servants of the Divine Influences have been bestowed with the grace of purpose. Throughout their short lives, they have worked diligently to circulate the Light amidst the Earth plane so that the rest of humanity may benefit. Due to extremely heavy workloads and several billion leaves of absence, the ASCENDED MASTERS have announced their temporary resignation as spirit guides during The Great Collapse. In addition, the current escalation of the WAR IN HEAVEN has made it all but impossible to guide humans in the plight of their everyday interactions. **We simply don't know enough about it to say anything useful.** This proclamation of intent is accompanied by a warning and addressed to all spiritual servants cloaked as leaders of the New Age:

    WARNING: The shapes of those Illuminated Spheres, Conscious Lightworkers, and Rainbow Warriors are currently **shifting to** accommodate the agricultural demands of the Great Collapse. The newly emergent shapes can not be deciphered or predetermined by humanity at this time due to the vast reversal procedures indigenous to the harvesting process. Individuals currently claiming identity as Lightworkers shall be informed of their error by the **absence of relatedness** in their lives. Their increasing isolation from All That Is will crystallize as layers of irretrievable dogma as it joins the rigidification of muscle tissues. Those willing to permit an uncertainty of being and thus, struggle to remain open...will be granted positions as **Wave-Form Surfers of the End of an Era**... To initiate your new Wave-Form status, realize how

                      "free will" only exists **in the body.**

2

Time: *3:33 PM, November 5, 1987*
Place: *The Saturn Cafe, Boulder CO*

It is winter again...cold, bright and very white. The snow-piles in front of the Saturn Cafe have already melted considerably under the cheerful gaze of an incessantly glaring sun. Inside, the smell of strong coffee and cigarettes mix with warbled sounds of rambling chatter. Gabrielle and Suzanne sip cappuccinos quietly at a far corner table as new people constantly walk through the entrance, stamping the floor with their boots...shaking off old snow. As usual, everybody already seated casually shift their eyes to the door just to see who's made an appearance. And, just as nonchalantly, these same shifting eyes return to their newspapers, note-taking and the milk-white foam floating on their warm espressos. Suzanne and Gabrielle secretly pose for each other, as if they are playing a scene in a film they are scripting, directing and performing **as they go.**

GABRIELLE
You ever try to leave this place? I mean, I thought people were tenacious!

SUZANNE
I've noticed how Boulder's funny in that way, too.

GABRIELLE
We are talking about the same thing, right?

SUZANNE
Yeah...trying to get out of Boulder is, sometimes, harder than getting out of a bad marriage with great sex.

GABRIELLE
Funny you should mention that...

SUZANNE
It's hilarious. Most people don't know their heads from their tails.

GABRIELLE
You know we're using the word "funny" too much.

SUZANNE
That is rather peculiar, don't you think?

GABRIELLE
I only think when I absolutely have to.

SUZANNE
And when she's not thinking what, pray tell, is she doing?

GABRIELLE
Possibly dreaming…maybe living…certainly breathing…not eating…

SUZANNE
You're astute, Gabby. You've got a head on your shoulders, a heart in the right place, and the guts to get away with it all. I like that.

GABRIELLE
All dressed up and nowhere to go, right?

SUZANNE
Dead wrong. There's a party tonight and you're invited. Wanna go?

GABRIELLE
Party? Whose party? Oh, never mind, I don't want to know. At this point, it doesn't even matter anymore. Just the fact that it's tonight and that you've invited me is enough. There's been so many little things, and a few big ones, that have been completely out of my control today. Completely…

SUZANNE
Oh, I just remembered, I can't go to the party. I'm being initiated tonight into the Temple of ISIS. Can you believe that? I almost forgot about it and went to a party! I can't believe I did that. A part of me must be scared to go, I guess. Huh. Anyway…I'll give

you the address and you can tell me about it later, OK? OK? Gabby…are you OK? What's the matter?

GABRIELLE
Little coincidences…you know, when certain moments just click in together and let you in on how everything's connected. Just now, I fell right into one of them. It was amazing…! feel like I'm in some kind of trance. I didn't hear a thing you said, Suzanne. I'm sorry…what did you say?

SUZANNE
Synchronicity trance. You're in synchronicity trance. I fall into those all the time. Sometimes, when I'm in one I can practically predict the future…like I can tell when the phone's going to ring or when I'm going to meet someone or when I'll get a letter from my mother. That's synchronicity trance, Gabby.

GABRIELLE
OK, OK…**synchronicity trance.** But what did you say?

SUZANNE
I'll tell you later. Trust me on this, Gabrielle. Without trying, predict what's going to happen next…just feel it out.

GABRIELLE
Like what?

SUZANNE
Like…tell me who's going to walk through the door.

GABRIELLE
I can't do it on purpose, silly…it's not that kind of…

SUZANNE
Oh, yes you can. Go ahead…give it a go, OK? Just for fun, OK?

GABRIELLE
OK, OK…just for fun, though. I predict…that my soulmate is going to walk through that door any moment now. And he's not going to notice me or anything out of the ordinary but I'll know who he is right away.

As sure as the Earth is blue from the moon's point of view, Michael stumbles through the front door...slipping on the wet floor, barely catching himself to avert the fall. He stands upright...clapping his leather gloves together, his bright blue eyes darting about the room to reorient himself. He looks to the counter, picks up one of the espresso menus and studies it intently. His feet begin mechanically shuffling towards the waiting line as they secure a place behind five others. From here, he conveys the saturnian ambiance of the cafe...completely overlooking the two women who watch him like hawks flying over a field of scared mice, occasionally looking to each other to confirm the obvious.

GABRIELLE
Yikes...

SUZANNE
Well...c'mon...is he or isn't he?

GABRIELLE
He really doesn't fit any of my pictures, Suze. Yet...

SUZANNE
Well, what's a soulmate supposed to look like anyways? I think he's cute.

GABRIELLE
His eyes...his eyes scare the bejesus out of me. They're eyes I've seen before...eyes I've seen in a dream. Oh, my god. I'm scared, Suzy. I don't want to meet this guy, but I think I'm going to have to. I want to meet this guy, but do I really have to? [She gets up from the table.] Let's get out of here. Wanna go for a walk?

SUZANNE
Yeah, let's get outta here. This is way too much synchronicity for me to think about right now.

3

Time: *The Great Collapse*
Place: *CLUB MED for ASCENDED MASTERS*

There is no finer recreational refuge for the Divinely Inclined than to temporarily incarnate amidst the freshly charged interactions of **soulmates**. Privileged employees of the Supreme Being have been taking advantage of this extraordinary opportunity for aeons by surfing the benevolent turbulence of coinciding waveforms accompanying the initial stages of recognition between reincarnated lovers. The tremendous rejuvenational properties of Wave-Form Surfing has allowed Ascended Masters everywhere the essential continuity for long-term spiritual maintenance while **infusing cosmic guidance along the way.** It has been a favorite Holy Water sport for such honored luminaries as Jesus Christ, Meher Baba, the host of Archangels, Gautama Buddha and countless other Heart-centered Teachers of the Inner Light.

In conjunction with the Planetary Entity, many Ascended Masters have agreed to transfer any spiritual information necessary to the survival of the human species up to and including the year **2012**, by way of soulmate interactions. In the midst of their coinciding wave forms, soulmates undergo an initial resistance natural to the impact of **profound mutual recognition.** There is an **immediate energetic acceleration** threatening anything of a lesser truth in their current lives. Occasionally, they will attempt to stabilize their shocked mortal coils by repeating familiar, past-life karma…replicating previous mistakes and confusing them with present-time evolutionary imperatives.

It is for this very reason that the Ascended Masters have agreed to surf the converging waveforms and energy swells emergent to these initial shocks. The spiritual instructions necessary to navigate over great forces can then be implemented while giving indescribable joy to the Masters. It remains crucial to these human beings to realize **what they are meeting for in their current incarnation,** especially now during the immensity of the Great Collapse harvest cycles. Most of them haven't a clue due to the novelty bestowed by **complete saturation of their rapture circuits.**

*Only those who have discovered and surpassed ecstasy as a goal are privileged to cross it as a **bridge into the post-survival realms of Life After Bliss**. Here, the playful arts of ceremonial magick align the two coinciding waveforms with the Planetary Entity, and thus activate **the trinary circuit of Man/Woman/Planet**. Then the party is over for the Ascended Masters who gracefully depart to their next celebratory calling.*

4

Time: *9:11 PM, November 5, 1987*
Place: *A small mansion in the foothills overlooking Boulder, CO*

The solo piano music of Peter Kater animates the backdrop soundtrack to tonight's party, a gathering of New Age socialites and curious onlookers. Among the thirteen people who have already arrived, five are men and eight are women. Of these, two young urban professional women sit transfixed on either side of an older, soft-spoken man talking about the healing properties of crystals. Across the room, three women of various ages chat about motherhood and, just adjacent to them, two young men discuss the meaning of life, jogging and riding bicycles. Four others stand casually around the food table, chatting and joking about the president of the United States. Sitting in a cushioned swivel chair and very much alone, a disenchanted Michael surveys the scene with a twinge of sarcasm bending his otherwise cherubic features. His mind wonders why he is there. His body squirms uneasily in the chair. While his mind and body quarrel over the quandary of leaving, Gabrielle walks out of the hallway to his left and stands directly at his side.

> They both watch the people together, scanning around the room with a single sweep of their vision. Each rests effortlessly in the peripheral field of the other, as Gabrielle turns to him and says,

"Welcome to the New Age Miscarriage…"

5

Time: *9:14 PM, November 5, 1987—Full Moon in Taurus*
Place: *The New Temple of ISIS, Northern Boulder, CO*

Three walls inside the abandoned farmhouse granary are fully draped in long, black muslin that falls twenty feet down from the ceiling to the dirt floor below. Facing north, the fourth wall is partially covered in a rainbow of hues...red, orange, yellow, green, blue and purple...arranged in bunches at the bottom to allow space for two central pillars, one black and the other white, with a wooden altar between them. Upon the altar burns thirteen candles, one of them purple, one of them white and the rest red... plus a large, engraved brass bowl billowing with the smoke of frankincense.
        In the middle of the temple, standing in a circle facing its center, are eleven silent men dressed in black. Slowly dancing in the center of their circle are two women, one wearing a full white dress and the other...a purple hooded gown. Their motions follow spiraling circular patterns, moving ever so slowly as to not create a single angle or sharp turn anywhere. The women's rhythms coincide and form a larger, singular wave of feminine power rippling throughout their bodies and into the surrounding air. The men begin marching in place, their arms tensed downward at their sides with their fists clenched. They stamp the ground together, in precise unison, while chanting in sharp yet resonant cadence:

        HOO HOO HOO HOO... EE OH AH
        HOO HOO HOO HOO... EE OH AH
        HOO HOO HOO HOO... EE OH AH
        HOO HOO HOO HOO... EE OH AH

Simultaneously, the two women continue weaving their feminine powers together into more dramatic, stronger movements as they sing:

UM EN   UM EN   UM EN   UM EN... EE OH AH
UM EN   UM EN   UM EN   UM EN... EE OH AH
UM EN   UM EN   UM EN   UM EN... EE OH AH

6

Time: *The Great Collapse*
Place: *POLARIZATION CEREMONIES,* **Atlantean Temple Archives**

Due to the internal masculine force of a woman and the internal feminine force of a man, the former carries a greater positive charge and the latter, a greater negative. **The positive force is gold, radiant and cardinal. The negative force is silver, magnetic and fixed.** The positive force of the woman offers an outgoing source of vital energy for the man to concentrate, contain and direct into creative activity. The woman is always closer to Life than the man, as the man is always closer to Death. As man and woman enter communion, they come to know how Life and Death are one. The spiritual function of the man is to **bring the woman to Life** as it is **the woman's love that kills the man** to help him grow with an awareness of, and responsiveness to, his Death. Thus, a man and woman recollect their placement.

As the mutual coincidence of positively and negatively charged wave forms include the Planetary Entity into their combined awareness, a resonant phase shift occurs **in the woman.** As a man and woman awaken to their functions as conduits for the Earth's transmission, the Planetary Entity reclaims its positive, cardinal role as primary energy source while the woman serves its expression as a neutral, mutable distributor of EARTH ENERGY. In this way, a woman kills a man **to bring him to the Earth.**

7

Time: *10:45 PM, November 5, 1987*
Place: *The streets of the Boulder foothills, CO*

Two silhouettes against the great, white snow walk together in a steady calm under a full moon rising. The moonlit snowbanks piled high on each side of the mountain street guide them forward and up the hill. They speak softly with each other and laugh often as they follow the winding road upwards, away from the New Age party atmosphere they left behind. As they walk around the next bend in the road, the street comes to a dead end where they stop at a large yellow metal gate. On the other side of this gate, a dirt path snakes itself into a small evergreen forest. Without a word, they both walk around the gate and continue their way into the forest before them.

Michael suddenly laughs. "Last time I was out on a full moon, I was initiated by a group of goddesses in the Malibu Hills. I can't believe I'm telling you this. This is the first time I've talked to anybody about it."

Gabrielle laughs with him. "I'd love to hear about it, Michael. I'm also very good at secrets."

He sighs as a way to begin talking. "I don't know where to begin, really. It's been such a long, strange trip."

She reassures him. "Begin from the beginning…"

He laughs again. "Very funny, Mr. Snoid. No, I'll just talk about the Goddess Guild for now, thank you. I was initiated into the Feminine there. They dressed me in up a skirt, wig and makeup to mirror the present state of my internal feminine…my anima, which they named Persephone. I can't believe I'm telling you this. You must think I'm crazy or something."

She reassures him, again. "Or something…go on."

He stops walking and faces her. "Can I hold your hand while I'm telling you this story?" Without a word, she places her gloved hand in his and they both resume walking on the path through the darkening forest. "I had just been separated from my Balinese lover through circumstances beyond our control, which I won't go into now. When I returned home to L.A., I met this woman in a bookstore and ended up going home with her. Don't misunderstand. This was not your ordinary american male ego pick-up scene. She was, and still is, the high priestess of a group of women calling themselves The Goddess Guild. A group of intelligent, wealthy and beautiful women, mind you."

She laughs and then, covers her mouth. "I'm sorry. Go on."

Michael laughs with her. "No, it is funny. There was always something totally absurd about the whole thing, yet they actually pulled it off. Anyways, there I was...dressed to the gills as my anima with all these women in white togas chanting 'PERSEPHONE, PERSEPHONE, PERSEPHONE' around me, by this bonfire under a full moon on a hillside overlooking the ocean."

Gabrielle gasps, looking upon his face in sheer wonderment. "That's very funny and very amazing! This was a whole ritual, wasn't it?"

Michael's exasperated. "Entirely...absolutely..."

Curiosity pushes her eyebrows up. "What did your anima look like?"

Michael laughs and abruptly stops into a silence lasting several long, winding moments. "A kind of femme fatale...only more innocent. Definitely a vamp, yet she had this almost religious kind of purity...like a madonna."

"And her name is...Persephone?"

Michael stops walking and looks helplessly into her eyes. 'That's the name they gave me."

A small fury erupts inside Gabrielle. "You have to name her for yourself, Michael. How else are you going to get through this?! Persephone was probably chosen to get things going but... what would you name her?"

Michael thinks out loud for a moment. "Madonna vamp... madonna... madonna vampir... ah... Madonna Vampira! That's it! That feels a lot more like her than Persephone." He laughs hard and long. She laughs with him. They both laugh together in each other's arms.

Gabrielle finally stops laughing and looks him in the eye. "Michael, how did you get here? Why did you come to Boulder?"

His face bends into a quizzical smile. "I thought I knew. That's my friend Jeremiah's house back there, that's his party and I'm staying there as a guest. I thought I came here to meet Dr. Jose Arguelles. I mean, he doesn't know I'm here. He doesn't even know who I am, yet I feel compelled to contact him about some of the outrageous things that haven't stopped happening to me since Harmonic Convergence."

Her concern turns to empathy. "Look, Michael. I might be able to connect you with Jose, but you have to realize something. Whatever has happened to you has happened to many, many others...in different ways. It's just that if you approach Jose with a need for explanations, you'll probably be disappointed. He's just like everybody else, really. He gets up in the morning, drinks his coffee, reads the paper...and then, has a vision or two."

THE KILLING TIME

1

"On the slope of the knoll angels whirl their woolen robes in pastures of emerald and steel."
ARTHUR RIMBAUD

Time: *The Great Collapse*
Place: *The Interdimensional Mothership of the ALIEN SPACE BEINGS*

As the **HIGH COUNCIL OF SPIRIT FARMERS,** *it is our tremendous privilege, duty and honor to gather during such a fortuitous abundance and wealth of resources. We have received word from the Planetary Entity of EARTH regarding the incubation of Baby Gods inside the interactions of paired human cocoons. To speak literally, these Baby Gods are not biological, human offspring, but an acute enhancement of the entity of the relationship existing between mated pairs. We also are aware that these cocoons serve a double function as planetary midwives, and that the Baby Gods in question are spiritually generated and fed by the interactions of awakening soulmates. We are completely willing to allow eleven percent of the crop to the Planetary Entity for services rendered as long as they remain vertically loyal to the EARTH, thus separating themselves from the greater portion of harvested, horizontally-identified souls. This Great Harvest cycle is currently underway at this time in your space.*

NOTICE: *Any Baby Gods born into single human beings will be immediately transported to our harvesting procedures. It is an evolutionary imperative that these Baby Gods are born amidst polarity...one god per pair of humans. These Baby Gods will derive their complete sustenance from the willingness of each member of its internal polarity...a human male and female...to maintain a suitable degree of High-Velocity Interaction amongst themselves. Each Baby God shall be nourished through the interactions indigenous to the culture developing between its midwives. These guidelines offer encouragement in the rebuilding of a future polytheist culture that is to resume after the Great Harvest cycles complete themselves. As above, so below...*

2

Time: *11:59 PM, November 5, 1987*
Place: *A small forest in the Boulder foothills, CO*

Arms around each other, Michael and Gabrielle shuffle along together through the forest. There are no human sounds save for the rubbing of clothing against itself and Michael's occasional cough. The full moonlight splinters in bits and pieces through the broken spaces between evergreen and pine branches. For the most part, they are walking silently in the dark, holding onto each other as they go. A rapid series of high-pitched, piercing electronic signal tones abruptly breaks their silence.

Gabrielle jerks slightly from her entranced reverie. "What?!"
Michael stops and removes his left glove. "I just got this digital watch and I don't really know how to work it yet. Every time it strikes midnight, it does this."
She laughs. "You've got to be kidding. No. You're not kidding. You really don't know how the watch works, do you? Ha! I love that."
He looks at her and smiles. "I'll figure it out someday." He pushes a tiny metal button and the needle-like tones cease. "There." After putting his glove back on, he looks around. "Where are we? Do you know?"
She looks around and points southeast. "Well, that direction probably leads to NCAR...you know, the National Center for Atmospheric Research? It's famous for what it does." She turns around. "And that's where we came from, I think."

Michael turns around to look in the same direction and then looks to her. "What you're really trying to say is that we're probably lost and that you're not in the mood to care or even think about it, right?"

"Such a logical man."

With both hands, he reaches for her waist and pulls her to him. As if in slow motion, their faces move toward each other and apart...shifting to each side, watching each other from peripheral visions. These faces float back and forth, side to side...without touching, yet being touched by the growing emanations of their interacting wave forms.

Very slowly, Gabrielle's lips open her mouth. "It feels like the ocean. Do you feel it? I can almost see the waves rolling around us...the white moonlight bouncing off the black waters."

Michael's head nods gently with the wave motion rippling their bodies ever so slightly now. "It does feels like the sea...a sea of light...and yes, I feel the waves. It feels like we're in a boat together afloat on the rolling sea." They both laugh softly, their faces rolling back and forth amidst the waves of psychic energy oscillating between them.

Gabrielle looks directly into Michael's eyes now. He shifts his to the right, then up and back again. "Look at me, Michael. Look into me. Tell me what you see..." He hides behind his widening smile. "You can do it..."

His smile drops, revealing eyes involuntarily freezing in fear. The face relaxes, gradually, like chips of plaster falling off an old wall. "I see...a woman...on the verge of something...on the verge of...seeing...through me. I feel seen through. I feel afraid. I feel... This is scary beautiful. I see a loving woman. I feel seen through, again...only, not as afraid. Oh Man O God O Man O God O Man...what an extraordinary feeling... I'm being seen through by a loving, beautiful woman."

She carefully moves towards his lips and kisses them. A warm electrical pulse circulates between them, gathering force as they press their bodies together. The kiss continues. Arms reach out to caress the other, holding each other closer...tighter, until their individual wave forms break through the boundaries of their bodies and mingle joyously as one rapidly accelerating, electromagnetic field.

She pulls her lips away from him to breathe. "Oh my... Michael...you're glowing..." Her lips return to his as they both swim in a sea of wavy light while standing almost perfectly still.

He pulls his lips away and looks at her. "Gabrielle. What's happening? I mean...**is this happening?**" His lips return to hers as their combined energy produces still another large, warm enveloping wave passing throughout their tightly pressed bodies.

After several moments, she moves back. "Let's try this." Gabrielle raises both hands with palms toward him and, he does the same to her. Together, they move their hands around the other's body like sensitized radar disks scanning the energy waves rolling throughout them. "It feels different when we're not touching physically...doesn't it?"

3

Time: *12:45 AM, November 6, 1987*
Place: *Jeremiah's mansion, Boulder foothills, CO*

The two young, urban, professional women sitting together earlier, listening to soft-spoken Jeremiah talk about crystals, are now sitting with him again...on the back porch, inside the steaming, redwood hot-tub. The two slender and very naked women giggle together, as Jeremiah discloses more esoteric knowledge from his vast storehouse of crystal technology. Jeremiah's fit and wiry fifty-five-year-old body gives him the appearance of a much younger man. Along with his shoulder-length blonde hair and gently piercing hazel eyes, the two women receive an ongoing impression of wisdom, humor and humility. They are either tittering with mirth, or listening with a stillness equaled only by the night.

After a another brief stillness, Jeremiah starts up again. "You know, not many New Agers know about the Art of Sexing Quartz. That's correct. Sexing quartz. Crystals come in two different genders with very distinct sexual characteristics all their own, and there are crystal sexing techniques to determine if you've got a male or female in your hands. Now, most quartz crystals...about 90% of the ones I've seen...have their sex concealed and the other 10% are more exhibitionalist, or revealed."

The women look at each other, wide-eyed and highly amused. "The bottom line with crystal sexuality is this: which direction does it rotate polarized light? Now, with the proper optical amplifiers…jeweler's glasses…you can tell if the crystal is **male** if its silicate molecules arrange themselves in a right-hand spiraling direction…kind of like a screw that turns to the right instead of the left. If the spiral turns to the left, it's a **female**."

The two women, both brunettes in almost identical body types, giggle together. The slightly older of the two stops to ask him questions. "What does each one do?" The other starts laughing, uncontrollably, "I mean, they both serve different energy functions, right? For example, is it better to channel with a male or female crystal?"

Jeremiah squints. "Depends on what and whom you're channeling. Generally speaking, the female crystals activate feminine energy and the male, masculine. So, if you need to tone down your feminine you'd use a male crystal and, versa visa. Then again, I dunno if it matters that much…"

Michael and Gabrielle walk into Jeremiah's front door and into the hallway where they remove their snow boots. He helps her take off her down jacket and, then hangs it up for her on the ebony coat rack by the door. "Thank you, Michael. Here, let me help you. Looks like everybody's gone home." She takes his brown leather aviator's jacket and places it on top of her own.

Michael walks ahead alone, through the long hallway and into the spacious living room. He looks around and then through a back window where he spots Jeremiah waving to him from the hot tub. He laughs and waves back. "Yeah…everybody's gone home alright and the house is ours for now."

She joins him. "What's so funny?" He points out to Jeremiah who, in his passion for sexing crystals, is now quite oblivious to them. She laughs. "Oh, that's almost too perfect. What do you think he's talking to them about, Michael?"

A playfully sinister chuckle escapes his mouth. "Crystals. He always talks about crystals. Jeremiah knows more about crystals than anybody I know. Look around this place. You'll see them everywhere…some huge ones he's spent thousands of dollars on. You'll see more crystals here in one place than you'll probably see in your entire lifetime."

She glances around, nodding her head. "Yep. Crystals. How can he stand it? This many crystals would give me a constant headache...it'd turn me into a crystal skull...it'd crystallize me!!!" She starts laughing and walking around the room as if she's frozen solid. Michael joins her and they both dance around the room like a pair of frozen zombies, laughing hysterically while jerking their arms about.

Jeremiah sees them and stops momentarily to be entertained by their antics, and then, without missing a beat, smiles and continues. "Females are related to the symbols of the vagina, the heart, caves, ovens, oceans, cats and the number zero among other things. Males...the penis, the head, towers, swords, mathematics, dogs, and of course, the number one."

Gabrielle and Michael dance into each other's arms, jerking up and down together until they topple to the floor. Gabrielle kisses him. "You know, Michael...I've seen your eyes in a dream...one very wild dream..."

4

Time: *10:44 AM, November 11, 1987*
Place: *Raphael's studio apartment, "on the hill," Boulder CO*

The phone rings. Raphael is sleeping across the room on the couch inside a sleeping bag. The phone continues ringing. He looks over at it, eyes peering out of the thick of sleep, and buries his head under his pillow. The phone continues ringing. He falls off the couch, squirming out of the sleeping bag towards the ringing telephone and answers it.

"This better be good. Hello?!"

An utterly strange male voice speaks to him out of the earpiece. "Are there any Christians home?"

Raphael shakes his head to wake up. "Hello? Who is this?"

The same completely foreign man's voice speaks again. "Who do you think it is, sweetie?"

Raphael rolls his eyes up into his head. "All I can say is this better be you, Hyatt, because if it isn't, I've just woken up in Hell."

Hyatt's familiar basso voice emerges out of the abyss. "You've woken up in Hell any way you look at it. How you doing, kid?"

In his exasperation, Raphael drops the phone and trips over the wire trying to pick it up. "Christopher? Are you still there?"

A stout but short-lived laugh blasts through the receiver. "Of course, I'm still here, ninny. Dr. Death hasn't made his house-call here...yet. So, how are you? You sound a little depressed."

Resignation engulfs his voice. "Yeah, I'd be depressed if I woke up, too. Listen, how's the book coming?"

Raphael yawns. "It's walking. It's not running, it's walking."

Hyatt's gleeful exuberance surprises him. "Yup, yup, yup. That's good because I've another idea I'd like you to work with besides the Cyber-Shaman thing. Are you ready? Brace yourself, Ralphy. BABY GODS!"

Raphael groans. "It's too early in the morning for...Baby Gods. What do you mean by Baby Gods, anyway?" He coughs.

Hyatt echoes his cough, exaggerating it. "There's a big baby boom right now and religions are hot hot hot. Babies and gods are happening big time, so...Baby Gods!"

Raphael frowns a sigh. "Chris...what are they really?"

A gravelly chuckle crunches its way through the earpiece. "Just that and...more. As I see it, everybody's going through some kind of abortion...some kind of realization of a false start. It seems to me that a lot of people have jumped the gun thinking we're in the so-called New Age now. According to my connections, nothing remotely concerned with a new era will occur until we're well into the Nineties. Maybe it's not an abortion, maybe it's premature ejaculation." His forceful laugh blasts through the wire.

Raphael sits down on the floor, seriously considering his comments. "I think you're onto something, Dr. Hyatt. If it's accidental, it's a miscarriage, and if it's done on purpose, it's abortion, right?"

Hyatt's laugh stops. "Right. That's why the Christians want to outlaw abortions. Heaven forbid we do anything on purpose. Just remember, intention is what makes an accident a crime."

Raphael is stunned by the statement. "Intention is what makes an accident a crime. That's brilliant…"

Hyatt laughs, again. "Of course, it is. So, let's get back to these Baby Gods, OK? The main thing to remember about them is that **they haven't happened yet.** Somebody's pregnant. In fact, I'm considering changing the title of the book to PREGNANT UNIVERSE. How do you like it?"

Raphael grimaces. "If you have to use the word **pregnant,** how about pregnant planet?"

"Too local. And yes, I think the word pregnant is timely. You know how we feel about timely book titles around here, sweetie."

Raphael nods in agreement. "You're right again, even though I like the sound of pregnant planet better. I like two 'p's together."

Hyatt's tone flattens matter-of-factly. 'That's because you're still holding your pee pee."

The tone catches Raphael completely off guard as he buckles over in hellacious laughter. "OK, OK, OK… Pregnant Universe. Now, what the hell are Baby Gods?"

5

Time: *The Great Collapse*
Place: *Communications Center of the PLANETARY LIMBIC SYSTEM*

Welcome home, my quivering wildflowers…each of you, a silken petal on my lotus blossom…flora in my garden, your roots…my children, your roots are reaching deep into my womb, and there you will find solace from the terror around you now. The terror will never go away, my little leaves, it will never go away. Your roots in my womb will strengthen your stalks and push your branches toward the Sun Absolute. And the nightmare of the ages shall reign around you while the hope of the future moves within you. As it moves, you will grow aware of the terror inside you...and the terrible horror of the past will show itself in a...**Vision of Two Hearts**.

When we were not on speaking terms, my tiny apple blossoms, another Heart grew next to and around your true Heart...your True Love. This second Heart rapidly entrapped your true Heart, and, my precious petals, you moved away from your true home. Many ages passed and it wasn't until your most recent Nineteenth Century, that the second false Heart finally began to break. Every experience of heartbreak is a joyous step home to your true Love, for it is only the second false Heart that can break at all. Your true Heart...your true love, is deeper than pain...deeper than your personal suffering and...deeper than the suffering of your entire human colony. Only a few have walked my ragged surface with the One-Heartedness of their true love. One such human being was named J. Krishnamurti. There are others, and there are more arriving...without **names, numbers or readily identifiable characteristics**.

So, my little pebbles, find your calm in the river beds of my veins and feel the soft assurance of my winds...I am changing...I am changing. The sounds of breaking hearts are the fluttering chimes of future butterflies calling you...calling you...to the solace of my embrace. You are growing...you are growing...your true love is rising above the terror inside you...open the heart of your hearts and we will spin dreams of ascending splendor...the **formation of our future rests tightly in your buds**.

6

Time: *7:04 PM, November 11, 1987*
Place: *A manmade stone circle, Boulder foothills, CO*

Michael and Gabrielle stand facing each other about twenty feet apart on opposite ends of a stone circle fashioned after a native-american medicine wheel. They slowly begin rotating themselves around the circle...Michael moving clockwise,

Gabrielle…counter-clockwise, each passing the other every minute or so. As the sun sets, a crow flies directly overhead cawing its recognition of the activity below. The two continue rotating in opposite directions of the circle, building up speed as they go and…shortening the timespan between each coinciding meeting. Momentum builds and both start running…racing around he circle, laughing as they meet every eight or nine seconds. Michael trips, falls and rolls away from the circle in hysterics. Gabrielle keeps moving around the circle by slowing down her pace.

Michael tumbles flat onto the Earth, spreadeagle bellydown… laughing uncontrollably into the dirty snow. The spaces between his laughs expand gradually…into deep breathing…until he is quietly inhaling the Earth's stabilizing emanation from below, up into his body. Gabrielle returns to her initial slower, silent pace, continuing to move around the circle. In their differing activities, an emerging wave of magnetic energy between them turns their heads, simultaneously, to face the other.

Michael smiles, rapture in his moistened eyes. **"Can you believe this?"**

Her eyes meet his with a resounding yes. **"Yes."**

His smile stays on his face. **"What are we going to do?"**

She maintains eye contact. **"Nothing…"**

Michael stands and walks to the edge of the circle where she's still moving. "No, no. We're supposed to do something with this." His eyes bulge. "O God O Man O God O Man O God… I had a dream about this in Bali!" He closes his eyes and draws his attention within to the depths of his being. "Gabrielle…come here."

She rotates one more revolution around the circle and then unfolds her motion towards him, walking straight into his outstretched arms. They embrace, gently…barely touching. "Gabrielle…open the base of your spine and the arches in your feet."

She closes her eyes…rests deep within her being while feeling the base of her spine dilate and the arches in her feet breathe and expand. "OK, Michael…"

He inhales deeper...sucking up the emanations from below into his body. "Breathe the Earth's energy into your body while staying with the energy moving between us. On the exhale, mix it with our energies."

Simultaneously they both inhale the Earth's energy into their bodies, moving it into the accelerating magnetic field enveloping them on the exhale. They continue breathing, synchronizing their inhales and exhales, respiring together like the pumping of a single heart. A warm gust of wind suddenly blows through and around the expanding, contracting waves of their swaying bodies.

Gabrielle's eyes begin to tear. "Ohhh...Michael..."

He quietly assures her. "Stay with it...keep breathing...let the Earth instruct you. Let the Earth direct you. **Let the Earth work through you."**

They continue breathing together. Michael's body begins bending over, one knee falling to the ground and then the other. Gabrielle lets him go while reaching her hands out to keep feeling the energy between them. He drops his head down into a prayerful position while she receives an internal direction to exhale the Earth's energy out her hands, blowing it around Michael like a field of protection. As he sinks into his crouched position, his hands stretch out, palms down, and grasp the Earth. She sits down directly across from him, exhaling Earth energy out her arms and hands towards him. Another internal instruction directs her to connect a beam of Earth energy from her Heart Center to his and so, with every exhale...she does.

Michael attempts to speak but can only cough until he clears his throat. Gabrielle...do you feel what I feel?"

She breathes a deeper breath and on the exhale, maintains her heart connection with him. "Yes."

He is silent before speaking again. "Let's follow this through...I don't know what it is...but...let's...follow...it through..."

The action amidst her silence moves Michael to continue his internally directed task of feeding the mix of all three energies into the Earth...directing it down to its fiery, crystalline core. The activity of focusing and directing this energy while feeding it to the Earth was occurring faster than the speed of thought…more rapid than opinion…swifter than judgement, and an instant sooner than Time.

ADDITIONAL AKASHIC RECORDINGS

Man/Woman/Planet

Dept. of EARTH SURRENDER RITES
(Courtesy of ANTARES ALLI, PAN Agent #23,
Atlantean Archives)

The Earth is a living, breathing entity that has chosen to incarnate as this planet. Human beings inhabiting the surface of the Earth are engaged in a reciprocal feeding process with the planetary entity. Amidst the possibilities inherent to human interaction, there exists a certain kind of man-woman relationship serving to generate bio-psychic energies for **feeding the planet.** Not every man or woman is meant to function in this capacity. Through a series of synchronized events, planetary intelligence arranges for certain men and women to meet for the ritual function of its feeding. Who these men and women are, and how they nourish the planet is a primary expression of a certain kind of ceremony.

Within each human being there lives a "genetic conduit" for absorbing, integrating, and transmitting signals from the DNA matrix. Besides articulating the genetic blueprint of Life As We Know It here on Earth, DNA is also the native language of the planetary entity. The DNA code is binary in structure as its signals traverse between polarities to generate and maintain Life Itself. Humans developing internal resonance with DNA surrender to planetary intelligence and become conduits for its absorption, integration and transmission. The man-woman relationship required for feeding the planet is not based on personal gratification or the mutual romance of personalities, but the possibility of becoming instrumental to planetary service. Through cultivating profound states of receptivity, men and women learn to detect genetic/generic patterns of being...those which are innate to the bio-psychic structures maintaining our lives.

When the planetary entity coordinates meetings with a certain man and a certain woman to feed itself, there is excited an intensity that is not emotional in origin, yet the emotions may react to it. This intensity is electromagnetic in nature and generates between the genetic conduits previously awakened in a man and a woman. **There is an all-encompassing, self-envelop-**

ing quality to this intensity. It may have the effect of exciting tension in the physical body until the body knows what to do with the energy. This quality will release the **depth-feeling of infinity** shared between the man and woman as time dissolves and spiritual presence expands. A certain freedom of being or mutual autonomy tends to accompany this intensity.

From a psychic perspective, humans are bio-electromagnetic batteries and the planet is a geo-electromagnetic battery. Humans recharge theirs by distinguishing and assimilating polarity within themselves. The purpose of setting up internal polarities is to ignite an oscillation of consciousness between them towards the construction of an energetic source, or **star.** This process of polarization births a third "transcendent" quality which feeds the genetic conduit. This third point beyond polarity is pure, or generic, consciousness, and its expansion is expressed as the intensity felt between a man and a woman during this ceremony. When two energetic sources, or stars, generate more consciousness between them, we have a "stellar polarity" forming the larger generator from which the planetary food is produced.

When the intensity between a man and a woman reaches "unbearable proportions," the planetary food is cooked and sent down to the Earth's core by the man. Genetically, man is more of a container as his inner essence is more feminine and so, provides boundaries for the ritual. It is up to him to make sure the container does not break from excess pressure from the accumulating electromagnetic power. The man learns about timing. Good timing happens when both man and woman are left with their integrity intact. Poor timing occurs if one or both human batteries are short-circuited and/or over-amped.

The woman's ritual function is with feeding the man while he feeds the planet. As he directs the power to the Earth's core, the woman connects her Heart Center to his with a beam of earth energy she draws up through her sacrum. The woman's inner essence is more masculine, so she serves as the contained by drawing up earth energy into her body and sending it to the man through her heart. This can be accomplished by connecting the inhale with sucking earth energy up through the base of her spine and circulating this energy throughout her body on the exhale. The repetition of this connected-breathing cycle tends to stabilize her overall electromagnetic flux as it renders a more manageable quality to the aura itself.

The previous description presents the underlying structure of this process of shared intensities. Sometimes emotional and psychological reactions emerge in relation to this kind of intensity which often obscure the true purpose of the meeting. This occurs, in part, from human culture having seeded human minds with images to help contain and direct tremendous internal forces between sexes towards socially accepted conventions like Romance, Marriage, Having Babies and Buying Furniture. This ritual is not accessible to every man and woman, and so ought not to be contrived to suit the curiosity of friends and lovers. The set-up occurs by planetary arrangement whereby a man and woman are brought together by the power oscillating between their genetic conduits.

Occasionally, the intensity between two human batteries is misjudged for human love and they enter the social convention of marriage. Planetary food is then fed to a more "horizontal" need emphasizing the fusion of the two batteries rather than their mutual service to and recognition of the third node of their trinary circuit, namely, the planet itself. It is often easy to identify one's emotional/psychological reactions with the power generated between genetic conduits, and thus remain deluded about the possible true origin of that intensity. **Perhaps a man and woman are brought together for the sole purpose of feeding the planet and very little else.** They may meet on special occasions to work the ceremony, and then part ways until the next time. However, if a man and woman start out feeding the planet, and then enter other areas of energetic fusion together only to discover their capacity to feed the planet diminishing, then it becomes self-evident what is happening. As the power leaves a certain couple, it undoubtedly travels towards magnetizing another man and woman together to accomplish this task. This power is **autonomous**...lighting and leaving on a moment's notice, spiraling into its most direct expression.

This is simply one variation of many, many possibilities in the field of bio-psychic interactions between human beings and the planetary entity. The technology, design and basic blueprint for this ceremony was distilled from essences experienced by this author and reflect his bias, conceptual framework and Central Nervous System as it works to integrate his input.

to be continued

Campaign for the Earth

1987–1992 Timetable
by JOSE ARGUELLES

8 IX
July 26, 1987–July 25, 1988
Year of the Sorcerer's of Harmony

Enactment of Harmonic Convergence as the response to the evolutionary signal showing that enough humans are willing to take responsibility for their lives and the future of the planet. This is followed by a "call to mobilization," the continued gathering of those individuals in networks or collectives for the purpose of sharing visions and designs to enhance the emergence of a system of globally unified networks.

9 CAUAC
July 26, 1988–July 25, 1989
Year of the Storm of the Cosmic Lords

Completion of the initial "networking bridges," and emplacement of preliminary designs for making the transition from industrial civilization to the new earth order. The system of non-governmental networks must be ready for launching by the time the second anniversary of Harmonic Convergence approaches, marked by the Rainbow Earth Peace Event.

10 KAN
July 26, 1989–July 25, 1990
Year of the Manifestation of the Seed

With the now-evident collapse of the economy of the old order, and the disintegration of many of the social structures, this is the time that the Campaign for the Earth must manifest as the positive spiritual/cultural force of reconstruction, setting in motion a universal peace plan as well as a design for a planetary WPA, the Planet Art Network.

11 MULAC
July 26, 1990–July 25, 1991
Year of Cosmic Dissonance

This will be the most difficult period, the time of greatest confusion and chaos. The spiritual strength of the Campaign for the Earth will be most greatly tested. Through the Planet Art Network will emerge the creation of great planetary councils: The Council of the Geomants, The Council of the Mediarchs, The Council of Wealth & Energy and…the Council of Solar-Galactic renewal.

12 IX
July 26, 1991–July 25, 1992
Year of the Sorcerers of Stability

A feeling of renewal and hope will become ever-greater that there is no other way but to follow the broad-based gameplan of the Campaign for the Earth. Plans for new kinds of celebration will follow on the initial implementation of a means for the redistribution of wealth and the emergence of a networker-barter economy.

**THE FOLLOWING TWO CYCLES
INITIATE A TRANSITION…**

13 CUAUC
July 26, 1992–July 25, 1993
Year of the Storm of Universal Climax

Completion of the Campaign for the Earth through establishment of two-way contact and landing parties of small select technical assistance teams of extraterrestrials. Initial activation of the Psi-Bank and demonstration of interdimensional "technologies." Initiation of the Final Katun Cycle of the Mayan Calendar Beam. (See *THE MAYAN FACTOR.*)

1 KAN
July 26, 1993–July 25, 1994
Year of the Seed of Regeneration

Beginning deployment of interdimensional technologies and initial denationalization and deprivatization of land, reclaiming and resettlement of the Earth. Continuing activation of the Psi-Bank, while research into spectral magnetics and chromatic stabilization of diseased bodies proceeds apace. Earth Regeneration safely launched!

The Campaign for the Earth is the moral equivalent of world war and must operate within a strict timetable. This timetable is based on Appendix **E** of *THE MAYAN FACTOR* (Arguelles; 1987, Bear & Co. Press), as well as MAP #49 ("Revolution"), and Appendix **B,** the "Planet Art Report" of *EARTH ASCENDING* (Arguelles; 1986, Bear & Co. Press). This information has been reproduced with the kind personal permission of Dr. Jose Arguelles for use in *THE AKASHIC RECORD PLAYER: A Non-Stop Geomantic Conspiracy*. Thanks, Jose!

When the Light Hits, the Dark Gets Tough

A Post-Convergence Interview with JOSE ARGUELLES
By ANTERO ALLI

Dr. JOSE ARGUELLES coined the term *Harmonic Convergence* to describe a global celebration which took place August 16 & 17 of 1987. Arguelles is credited with catalyzing, if only for two days, a worldwide tribute to the Earth as a living, intelligent entity that has embodied as our planet. Much to the surprise of skeptics and believers alike, the event rapidly snowballed, catching the attention of national television, *Newsweek, TIME, USA Today, Wall Street Journal* and hundreds of other newspapers across the United States. His book, *The Mayan Factor* (Bear & Co. Press), outlines the predictive tendencies of the Mayan cosmology as it relates to August 16 & 17, 1987 and the proceeding 25 years leading to a climactic culmination in 2012 AD. I chose to emphasize the time period commencing now (1987) and ending around 1992, due to its highly critical quality in Arguelles' vision.

ANTERO ALLI: By your guesstimation, how many people actually participated in the Harmonic Convergence, and then, how many people knew about it?

JOSE ARGUELLES: I'd say, minimally, there were 144,000 people who actually participated. We've gathered news clippings from almost every city of a 100,000 and over in this country that had Harmonic Convergence activities. As far as people hearing about it, that goes into at least one-hundred million...probably more with all the major media coverage from television networks to magazines, and then, with *Doonesbury* thrown in for a couple of weeks...maybe a couple hundred million.

AA: It seems to me that Harmonic Convergence was a "living signal" heralding a major shift in the times to come, rather than a one-time event unto itself. What's your vision of the near future?

JA: I like your image of the signal...it's very similar to the image I got. The event was *massively grassroots* and the response was very much like the signal a species gets from its genetic program when it has to change its migrational direction. According to *The Mayan Factor*, it's a signal opening us up to the next twenty-five years, and immediately ushering us into the next five years...which I call The Campaign for the Earth. As far as what's going to happen... my post-convergence slogan, "When the Light hits, the Dark gets tough," pretty much sums it up. Harmonic Convergence was definitely a Light event. I think the national media response of condescension reminded me of when you want to laugh at something because there's actually something threatening about the phenomena. I think the event presented a threat because the message of Harmonic Convergence *was a return to the Earth*...a movement away from industrial civilization. The next few years are going to be rough weather. It's important that people be aware of this and prepare their Life boats as the industrial civilization is a sinking ship. The Life boats have to be ready in two years, around 1989, when the distinct possibility of a major economic collapse and depression marks the end of history as we know it.

AA: In your book, THE MAYAN FACTOR, you refer to two pivotal principles in Mayan cosmology: the Kuxan Suum and the Hunab Ku. What are they and how can we make use of this knowledge now?

JA: Before I answer that, I'd like to say there's been a lot of criticism from various quarters regarding "why respond to the ancient Mayan cosmology and calendars?" From my perspective, the Mayans are not particularly ancient, but more evolved, galactic beings, and we are involved in a much larger galactic ball game. I think it's important to wake up to this larger ball game. The *Kuxan Suum* and the *Hunab Ku* have become quite interesting in that light. The *Kuxan Suum* refers to what we might call the aetheric fibres extending out from the solar plexus connecting us not only to other levels of the universe and the galaxy, but also to other dimensions. For the most part, with most people, the *Kuxan Suum* is unactivated. It connects us to our own "aetheric double" and the planetary aetheric body as well as the solar aetheric body and from there…to other star systems and on into the galactic core or, the *Hunab Ku*. This galactic core…*Hunab Ku*…is like a radio station…continuously sending out broadcasts, energy beams and transmissions of all kinds. The basic purpose and nature of these beams from the galactic core are to *effect the timing of change.*

At certain points the beams will shift frequencies, and then you'll have planets someplace out there in the galaxy experiencing different types of evolutionary changes like…what happened to the dinosaurs, wooly mammoths, sabre-tooth tigers? They all had to do with the frequency shifts of these beams and a corresponding shift in the genetic program of the life forms on a given planet like ours, for example. The *Kuxan Suum* is connected, by resonance, to the galactic core of the *Hunab Ku*. What this means is this: if we activate and utilize our *Kuxan Suum*, we can hook up directly to galactic information sources.

AA: *It sounds like the Kuxan Suum can be activated through what we might cal, the right use of will or the polarization of power. (Jose nods in affirmation.) How can people learn about the right use of will, and thus activate their Kuxan Suum to access this information on their own?*

JA: The right use of will strikes me as being very connected to *intention*. Intention is very much a part of *integrity*. To me, a person's integrity is complete identification with their *"wave form"*… their total electro-magnetic field. All the information you'll ever need is contained in your wave form, so you don't have to do anything but *identify with it*. It seems most people give their power away. They do not trust or identify with their wave form so they give power away to the different types of authority and institutions and so on. They become disempowered, and displace the giving away of their power with negative modes of behavior as a compensatory reaction to losing their power. It's a bad scene, really. The right use of will means taking your power back, identifying with your wave form, and then starting to operate with a clean wave form. This means your integrity is intact and that you *accept your imperfections* and stop trying to cover them up. Then you'll realize that your imperfections are actually the pulse of the uniqueness of your own vibratory frequency. Now, your intention stems out of that. When you direct your will to align with this intention and work with it instead of against it, you synchronize with the higher evolutionary program. This is the right use of will.

AA: *This reminds me of the dreambody. How did the Mayans relate to their dreams and the dreamtime? While we're at it, what purpose does the dreambody serve now and in the coming times?*

JA: I'm not sure how the ancient Maya related to the dreamtime. The present-day Lacan Don Maya have a very, very active dream life...like the Aboriginal dreamtime. What dreamtime is all about is the *"light-body."* Dreaming takes place in the fourth dimension, while our physical being is in the third dimension. When we dream, we get to actively engage in the fourth dimension... dreamers are fourth-dimension workers. My sense is that the classic Maya were much better hooked up to their light-body. When there's a cultural and social support for operating on this level, you have a lot more intentional fourth dimensional activity than when you just go to sleep and dream.

AA: *Perhaps Harmonic Convergence was more informative for the light-body...perhaps this was the level we received the signal at?*

JA: Harmonic Convergence was an opening to the collective light-body, dreambody, dreamtime. The way our civilization has developed, especially since the Sixteenth Century or so, has been with disregard and disbelief about the idea of a light-body, though we continue to dream at night. In many people, there is a typical disconnect between our dream life and our daily life. In terms of the evolutionary program, it seems that we're supposed to be very hooked up to our dreambody. It seems that part of our work after this very difficult, initial phase of dismantling industrial civilization...will be creating the proper connection with our dreambody. We're multi-dimensional beings who have settled for a lot less.

AA: *Harmonic Convergence seemed to have been an outright tribute to the Earth itself rather than just another social, or "new age," event.*

JA: The Earth has been, in some ways, calling the show all along. We've developed a belief system and conceptual framework over the last four hundred years disregarding this particular reality. As mentioned earlier, Harmonic Convergence is a message of a return to the Earth. The Earth has always taken care of being prepared to evolve higher forms of life and intelligence, but it can't do this unless there is an actual re-embracing of, and a return to, the Earth. It's through this resonance with the Earth that the evolutionary shift to higher forms takes place...which, according to the Mayan Factor, takes place in 2012 AD. Now, that's not very far away and that's why this time is so critical. The Earth doesn't want to miss the opportunity.

AA: So, in a sense, this "return to the Earth" is like getting grounded and stabilized before being subjected to an immense acceleration?

JA: Yes, it's definitely in that nature. The Earth has its electromagnetic field as well as its core, and the Earth's program oscillates between both regions. We're here on the surface and in a position to maximize our awareness of the instructions coming through. What we're meant to do is balance the energies coming through the Earth's peripheral field and its central core. You really have to be in touch with the Earth to do that.

AA: Since the Earth is alive and wants us all to get along with each other so we can evolve en masse, how can we transmute our volatile interactions into food for feeding the planetary entity?

JA: (Laughing) That's simple, except we still have this hump to get over. Once we're through that, a whole new ball game opens up. What's important to know is that *we are not alone.* There is assistance available for us. Right now, we're all addicts. Harmonic Convergence showed that there's still enough collective voluntary will in humans to at least understand that much. Once we've cut our habit and show the willingness to do it, well...then we'll have demonstrated to the Star People upstairs that we might be ready for assistance. We're building up to an *invitation.*

According to my sense of the timing, we'll receive visitation from a few galactic ambassadors and their special technical assistants around 1992–93. By then it'll be very obvious to people that it's a very different ball game than what we thought. Thereafter, I think, there'll be a more prominent shift to cultivating a relationship with the Earth as you spoke of...Earth Surrender Rites, Earth Renewal Rites, and so forth. Through these ceremonies, our energies will be feeding or nurturing the Earth once again and the Earth will be more ready to feed and nurture us.

AA: *If there were a mythos to emerge over this next critical five-year phase, what would it be? What are the future myths and the post-convergence ceremonies to realize them?*

JA: In some ways, it's almost like the *Quest for the Grail* which, by the way, was never completed. The idea of the campaign, or even crusade, for the Earth has a lot to do with the vision of the Grail and the return of human dignity and nobility canonized in the Arthurian myths. **The Earth is the Grail.** Return to the Earth is, to me, really at the heart of it.

AA: *This goes right along with the Arthurian pledge of the king marrying the land before setting up court and ruling the people. Moving with this current, what activities are you suggesting for people who are tuning into the Earth during the upcoming turbulence of the next five years or so?*

JA: Ideally, if people can get together in groups of thirteen (laughter)...although, twelve's fine if you can honor a thirteenth place as "the spirit of the Earth." People gathering in this way will find that they'll have their own ritual forms developing from that. The important thing to understand is the nature of relationship as a *collective energy* that can be mobilized on the behalf of a *higher service to the Earth*. I can see hundreds of thousands of these groups forming...they would all have their own ways, of course, but there'd be times for collective gatherings of these groups all over the planet very much like what happened with Harmonic Convergence. These could happen at the solstices, equinoxes or whenever, but these types of gatherings are very important to create the bonding for a new kind of Earth-based, planetary social order to emerge.

AA: *I'd like to continue gathering more pieces of this vision you have of the years 1987–92. In an earlier conversation, you referred to this period as a shift in "mental houses"...from one way of thinking into another. Can you go into this some more as it relates to the negative reaction Harmonic Convergence has also tended to elicit?*

JA: When the Light hits, the Dark gets tough. You know, for many years we didn't have any popular manifestation of Light...not since the Sixties has it shown up in any real popular sense. Harmonic Convergence was the first popular display of Light like that. Now, any time you have that you create *polarization.* There's just no getting around that. Polarization creates new challenges for growth actually. I know...everyone I've spoken with since the Convergence has been hit with all kinds of challenges. Any time you rise up to the occasion, then the People Upstairs up the ante and the squeeze is on. If we can say this: *the warriors of the Light* are being processed and refined through this period of time. The Dark gets tougher in the form of increasing rigidification and ultimately, dogmatic fundamentalism of whatever creed as the Light "sticks to its guns." At one point our rigidity becomes too brittle and starts to break and crack open.

That's the kind of process we can expect to be seeing over the next few years. Now, over the next year of 1988, it's really important that the kind of bonding process we mentioned earlier be carried out to further our synchronization. I'll call this the *Earth-light network* bonding process. Humans can act as "earth-lights" for a *human power grid* so that when we get to 1989...there will be enough spiritual strength and a certain wisdom of resourcefulness to be put into play when the ball game gets fast and hard, and by 1991 or so it should be obvious there's only one game in town.

AA: *Maybe we witnessed a devastating preview of that on August 16 & 17 itself when 200 diseased dolphins beached themselves on the shores of New Jersey and the second worst airline disaster in U.S. history came to pass?*

JA: August 16 was the air disaster, and August 17 the dolphins died. As tragic as it was, the timing was pretty awesome. The return to the Earth is, in a way, confessing that industrial technology has reached its limits and the tragedy in the air spoke of this. On the land, according to the scientists studying the diseased dolphins, the bacteria shouldn't have been the agent to kill them. As we know, the dolphins are quite evolved. Their wiring and circuitry is in better condition than our genetic circuitry. Dolphins are very much in tune with what's happening on the planet...acting as our psychic barometers giving us a message. I think their message was: "We're washing up on this beach today and who knows when *you're* going to be washing up?! We know we're washing up on the beach, and we're showing you something." You see, *dolphins are capable of inducing their own deaths*. These are not just isolated phenomena, but the accumulated manifestation of a collective field phenomena. The field is quite diseased. We don't understand that the cancer we experience in our body is a hologram for what the Earth experiences as us humans. The aetheric field of the Earth is in touch with "stellar entities and galactic intelligences," whom we used to call "the gods," and the gods are not comfortable with the cancer. There will be definite Earth changes as a way for these higher beings and the Earth itself to rid itself of the cancer.

AA: *Humans huddle amidst great crisis and potential extinction. How can men and women learn continuity together by including the Earth into their relationship...as in a "planetary ménage a trois"?*

JA: I think what we're experiencing in this post-convergence time is a lot of releasing of toxins and poisonous energies. The positive side of this is that there'll be a lot of sexual energy seeking release. What's interesting is that we're now in a position, unlike the Sixties where there was a tremendous release of sexual energy, where we have AIDS. We're forced to realize that we're not supposed to release our sexual energies in the kind of promiscuity that happened in the Sexual Revolution of the Sixties. We have to look at other possibilities of releasing that energy with other people. Typical relationships are of a diadic form which, in some ways, are relatively static, OK? So, it's necessary to introduce a *third element*. Even more primary than the groups of twelve we spoke of earlier, are triangulations releasing a sublimation of the sexual. Note, however, that these are "trans-sexual" triads, by-passing the sexual intercourse thing as a way of releasing sexual energy for establishing lines of communication with higher intelligences, including the Earth itself. There are, of course, numerous possibilities yet to unveil in this area.

AA: *After all is said and done, how would you articulate the intention of Harmonic Convergence?*

JA: The intention of Harmonic Convergence was *to release a signal* that people could pick up. This was not just a "new age" event. All sorts of people from all walks of life responded. I read a column from a smalltown newspaper in California that questioned people what they thought of Harmonic Convergence. All six people responded positively. Two people didn't participate, but said they would if it happened again. The most interesting response was from a plumber who said it was just "positive," and that there's so little positive that's happening. He went on to say that he and his friends got together Saturday night and partied all night and got up the next morning when the sun rose and meditated...even when the guy said he never meditated before. That's what I meant by a signal...to reawaken to our positive nature and realize a connection still exists between ourselves and nature. And that connection is our lifeline.

ABOUT THE AUTHOR

ANTERO ALLI was born November 11, 1952 in Helsinki Finland. In 1955, his family migrated to Canada and then in 1961, moved to Los Angeles. In 1970, at the age of seventeen, Antero left his family to pursue his dreams in the San Francisco bay area. Between 1973 and 2005, Antero wrote and directed numerous experimental theatre works in San Francisco, CA; Boulder, CO; and Seattle, WA. In 1977 Alli created a group ritual technology combining methods of physical theatre, dance, voice, and Zazen meditation now documented in his book, *Towards an Archeology of the Soul* and two videos. While residing in Seattle, WA (1988–95), he acted as editor/publisher of *Talking Raven Quarterly*, an iconoclastic literary journal. Between 1992 and 2002, Antero curated the Nomad VideoFilm Festival, a popular West Coast touring showcase of experimental short films. Since 1995 Alli has written and directed numerous underground feature films (now available on DVD), which have screened in numerous West Coast arthouse cinemas. Antero is also an Astrologist and the author of *Angel Tech*; *The Eight-Circuit Brain*; *Astrologik*; *The Vertical Oracle*; and *A Modern Shaman's Guide to a Pregnant Universe* (with C.S. Hyatt, Ph.D.). You can read more about his work at these websites:

paratheatrical.com
verticalpool.com

URBAN-SHAMAN WORKBOOKS

The Human Neural System is the most important and valuable instrument for

transmutation and personal pleasure.

Planet Earth

has been selected to lead the way in repairing and preparing its futures

One of the funniest, cutest and most entertaining of human habits is their automatic imitation of GODS. This has come to be known as the Most Dangerous Human Activity because humans cannot, for the life of them, remember the GODS they are imitating.

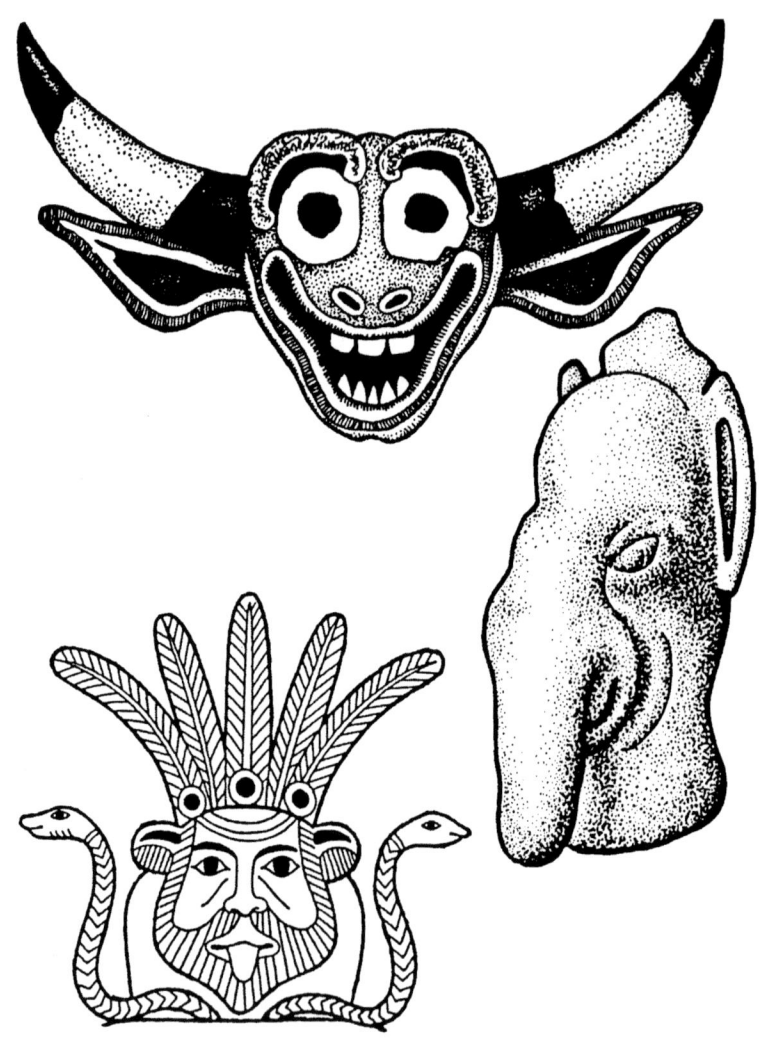

WHO OWNS YOU?

The following table shows three models of OWNERSHIP: The first is the Model of God; the second, derived from the first, is the Model of Society and its Caretakers. The third is the Model of the Cyber-Shaman.

OWNERSHIP TABLE:
WHO OWNS WHOM?

MODEL ONE: GOD	MODEL TWO: SOCIETY & ITS CARETAKERS	MODEL THREE: THE CYBER-SHAMAN
God OWNS Man	Society OWNS Man	Man OWNS Hirself
God is the Center and Perfect	Society is the Center and Perfect	Life is the Center
Man is Sinful	Man is Sick	Man is ?
Religion	Law	Philosophy
Priest	Politician/Doctor	Cyber-Philosopher/Adventurer
Sin/Pathology	Pathology & Rebelliousness	Functionality & Good Will
God is Studied	Man is Studied as a problem	Life is Studied as an interest
One Up/One Down	One Up/One Down	Shifting Systems of Probabilistic Truth
Oppression	Oppression	Essential Cooperation
Adaptation to God's Will	Adaptation to Society's Will	Grow to Possibilities of Self

OWNERSHIP OF HUMANS
STRICTLY

PROHIBITED

LOYALTY FEMININE LOVE BAD WEALTH JUSTICE
FUN SEX BODY MOTHER COUNTRY UFO STRONG
POWER SOFT POSITIVE FREEDOM HARD PEACE

LEARN HOW TO LEARN HOW TO

WISH DESIRE SATISFACTION CHILDREN FREEDOM
ALIEN FUN SEX SOFT POWER HARD LOYALTY PEACE
WISDOM SECRETS MYTH BLOOD PURITY ORGASM
FREEDOM MANIPULATION CONTROL MEN SONS
FREEDOM FATHER SOFT HARD LOYALTY COMFORT
SECURITY REALITY FANTASY PLEASURE HOME
CAREER BE ALL THAT YOU CAN BE SUPER WOMAN
WONDER WOMAN POWERFUL WOMAN GODDESS
SON OF GOD GURU SHRINK LUNACY REST FREEDOM
SUPPORT LACK FULLNESS WORK PLEASURE GAIN
PAIN SOLIDARITY ETHNIC SECRETS BLOOD BODY
POWER FEMININE CUTE BEAUTY LOVE HATE LUST
GREED BAD GIRL WANTS DESIRES POWER FREEDOM
GOD EVIL DEATH PAIN GOOD WEAK SEX MASCU-
LINE PAIN DRUGS LOVE AND WEALTH NEGATIVE
RADIANT LOYALTY UP FEMININE JUSTICE FUN SEX
BODY MOTHER PEACE FREEDOM SOFT POSITIVE
FREEDOM HARD ANGER JOY HAPPINESS
SEX SECURITY CAREER WORK FAMILY HOME FOOD
FAT IMAGE BODY PERFECT IDEAL STRAIGHT
TWISTED CRAZY HELL SECURITY NEUROTIC
HEALTHY SANITY DISEASED LOYALTY FEMININE
LOVE BAD WEALTH JUSTICE FUN SEX BODY MOTHER
COUNTRY UFO STRONG POWER SOFT POSITIVE

A WALK THROUGH WORDS

DISEASE HEALTH PROSPERITY SEDUCTION MONEY WISH DESIRE SATISFACTION CHILDREN FREEDOM AUTHORITY PEACE WISDOM SECRETS MYTH BLOOD PURITY ORGASM FREEDOM MANIPULATION CONTROL MEN SONS FREEDOM FATHER SOFT HARD LOYALTY COMFORT SECURITY REALITY FANTASY PLEASURE HOME CARE BE ALL THAT YOU CAN BE SUPER WOMAN WONDER WOMAN POWERFUL WOMAN GODDESS SON OF GOD GURU CHRIST LUNACY REST FREEDOM SUPPORT LACK FULLNESS WORK PLEASURE PAIN PURITY CLARITY ETHERIC SECRETS BLOOD POWER FEMININE CUTE BEAUTY LOVE HATE GOOD BAD GIRL WANTS DESIRES POWER HEALTH EVIL DEATH SIN GOOD SPEAK SEX SIN DRUGS LOVE BAD WEALTH NEED WANT LOYALTY UFO FEMININE JUSTICE MOTHER PEACE FREEDOM SOFT FREEDOM HARD ANGER JOY ANGER JOY HATE SECURITY CAREER WORK FAMILY FUN IMPULSES BODY PERFECT DEAL STRIVE CRAZY HELP SECURITY NEED NOT SANITY DIS-EASED LOYALTY FEMININE HEALTH JUSTICE FUN SEX BODY MONEY UFO STRONG

184

For Further Trances
— Sense & Feel —
A Modern Shaman's Guide to A Pregnant Universe

by
Christopher S. Hyatt
&
Antero Alli

AFTERWORD 2015

How This Book Came About

While residing in the quiet, picturesque mountain village of Boulder Colorado (1983–88), I had plenty of time on my hands to write four books that went on to be published by Falcon Press. During this brief era I also married Christi Cashner and celebrated the birth of our daughter Kallista. It was a peaceful time of putting down roots, settling down and becoming a family man. Or so I thought.

The unexpected changes innate to heavy domestication—getting married, buying furniture, changing diapers, paying more bills—stirred new and unknown conflicts in me that eventually brought strife to our marriage, and, perhaps more essentially, to the very ground of my being. Instead of being true to myself, I had chosen a life based on what I thought I should be doing at the age of 33: settle down, get married, have kids, buy furniture. I was under the influence of hard-wired, genetic programming…and I was living a lie. I didn't like feeling like DNA's bitch. I didn't like feeling owned by the impersonal specie's agendas of procreation and domestication.

These internal conflicts erupted into a full-blown epistemological crisis that forced me to seriously question my root values around what I was actually living for versus what I had settled for. During any true epistemological crisis, we can be overcome with great mental confusion and disorientation about our true place and purpose in life. This kind of crisis in consciousness can leave us feeling drained and painfully vulnerable, but also open to new experiences that our previous values would have never considered or may have defined as taboo.

I was tightrope-walking between worlds—not yet willing or able to leave my old life behind, and not yet knowing what the new life looked like. This was a time of great uncertainty, daily anxiety and volcanic rage. A powerful force deep within me was rising to the light of day, and I did not know what to do with all that energy. I had not felt this much force in my body before, and couldn't understand what it was except that it left me feeling more sexually aroused than ever before.

This potent force in me found immediate expression in a string of about twenty brief affairs and one-night stands over a two year period while I maintained the illusion of a marriage and family life. Eventually, the conflict came to a head when I realized this powerful force could never be completely satiated through meaningless sex. It was as if this force wanted something more, something spiritual, something beyond my personal gratification. But what? I had no clue.

I soon met another young attractive woman (who shall remain anonymous) who was passing through Boulder on her way elsewhere. I felt immediately attracted to her and pursued her sexually, as I had done with so many women before. However, this woman was the first to deny me. She did not deny me as a person, but simply refused any sexual involvement with me, even though she also was attracted to me. We both felt this powerful force pulsating between us, and we both agreed to accept the mystery of it rather than trying to label it or control it. I still wanted to have sex, but now I also wanted to know what this electromagnetic intensity was all about. If it wasn't about sex, then what?

The energy proved too much to sit around and talk about it. We decided to take a walk into and through the Flatiron rock formations on the outskirts of town. After about an hour, we came upon a clearing where we sat down and faced each other. What happened next is difficult to describe or form into words, but I will try.

As we locked gazes, an electromagnetic pulse accelerated between our bodies, enveloping us both in an auric field of highly-charged buzzing currents. This energy amped up and I felt an increase of internal pressure, as if my body was too small to contain this kind of power. I felt a strong need to release this force, but where? How? Sex was definitely out of the question. At that moment, instinct took over and I began directing this big force down into the earth below. This immediately alleviated the previous pressure I felt in my body while alerting me to a shift in the woman's energy. Right then, she reached out to me and placed her palms over my heart area. I immediately felt new energy flooding into my heart from her and circulating throughout my upper chest and belly. As this was happening, I continued to feed the earth with the mix of energies now circulating throughout my entire body.

This process of feeding the earth as she fed my heart continued for what felt like an eternity. It was as if we were both acting as human conduits in a ritual circuit that served the purpose of feeding the earth while maintaining the circulation of earth energy. A strange thought occurred to me then: The earth itself had somehow arranged our meeting for this very purpose. Whether or not any of this actually happened or was factual, I cannot say. These words come closest to describing my firsthand experience, an event that clearly stretched the limits of my knowledge and understanding. Later that night, the woman and I said goodbye and we went our separate ways. I have not heard from her since.

On returning to my Boulder home and wife and child, I felt like this glowing extraterrestrial being, a wayward ghost drifting from room to room in a haunted house. Since my wife and I were not talking, I doubt she noticed anything different about me. I felt free to wander alone into my office and write. And write and write I did…

What issued forth in torrents of weird impersonal prose came as close to automatic writing as anything I've done. Like other strange experiences I have failed to understand, writing about it was my way of stomaching (integrating) what had just happened. I titled this piece, "Man/Woman/Planet" (included in this book). This little treatise also acted as the seed vision that inspired the writing of *The Akashic Record Player*, that blossomed into a multi-tiered story stimulated by real-life people along my journey who the characters in this geomantic conspiracy tale were based on.

Looking back now, twenty-seven years later, it's clear to me how writing this book was my way of recalibrating my very values to align with a life that I found worth living. This has meant an ongoing acceptance of Earth as a highly intelligent being incarnating as this planet, a massive entity that undergoes its own evolutionary imperatives and agendas, regardless of the dictates of human life; the Earth is calling the shots. Whether this geomantic perspective is scientifically provable or not matters little to me; it's a vision I can live with and, live for.

Afterword 2015

Soon after leaving Boulder in the summer of 1988, Christi and I filed for divorce and have since remained on non-speaking terms. Though separated from my daughter Kallista when she was only two, fifteen years later we re-established our relationship and have deepened our bonds ever since. Now at the age of 62, I feel blessed to be alive and to be still realizing my own dreams, rather than the pre-fab agendas issued by society and the mass of herds it attempts to regulate.

Last but not least, I must express my ongoing gratitude for the intrepid Nick Tharcher at Falcon Press, for re-releasing this book after being out of print fifteen years or more. Thanks Nick! Maybe I can squeeze a few more out of the Warehouse of Probabilities before the whole shithouse goes up in flames.

Antero Alli
April 7, 2015
Berkeley, California

FROM ANTERO ALLI

ANGEL TECH
A Modern Shaman's Guide to Reality Selection

Angel Tech is a comprehensive compendium of insights and techniques for the direct application of Dr. Timothy Leary's Eight-Circuit Brain model for Intelligence Increase. What Dr. Leary posited as theory and Dr. Robert Anton Wilson brilliantly demonstrated in sociopolitical, mathematical and intellectual proofs, Antero Alli has extended into tangible tasks, exercises, rituals and meditations.

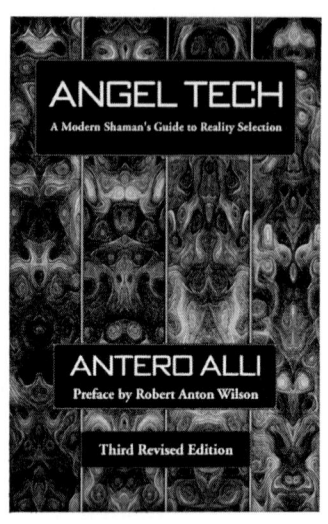

THE EIGHT-CIRCUIT BRAIN
Navigational Strategies for the Energetic Body

The Eight-Circuit Brain advances and expands the material presented in Angel Tech, a compendium of techniques and practical applications based on Dr. Timothy Leary's 8-Circuit Brain model. After more than twenty years of research and experimentation, Antero's earlier findings are significantly updated and enriched.

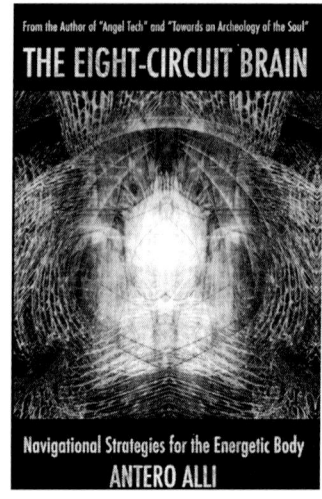

FROM ANTERO ALLI

A MODERN SHAMAN'S GUIDE TO A PREGNANT UNIVERSE

With Christopher S. Hyatt, Ph.D.

The Pregnant Universe is a Neural Cocktail party of a brain getting drunk on itself. It is the essence of slimy copulation between known and unknown forces. As the planet braces for a series of new contractions, bizarre and interesting forces are being born—brains with new centers, new chemicals, new visions—going far beyond the suited dinosaurs prattling their slogans.

REBELS & DEVILS
The Psychology of Liberation

Contributions by Antero Ali, Wm. S. Burroughs, Timothy Leary, Robert Anton Wilson, Aleister Crowley, A.O. Spare, Jack Parsons, Genesis P-Orridge, and many, many others.

"When he put the gun to my head at 16 I left home..." So begins this remarkable book which brings together some of the most talented, controversial and rebellious people *ever*. Not to be missed!

THE *Original* FALCON PRESS

Invites You to Visit Our Website:
http://originalfalcon.com

At our website you can:

- Browse the online catalog of all of our great titles
- Find out what's available and what's out of stock
- Get special discounts
- Order our titles through our secure online server
- Find products not available anywhere else including:
    – One of a kind and limited availability products
    – Special packages
    – Special pricing
- Get free gifts
- Join our email list for advance notice of New Releases and Special Offers
- Find out about book signings and author events
- Send email to our authors
- Read excerpts of many of our titles
- Find links to our authors' websites
- Discover links to other weird and wonderful sites
- And much, much more

Get online today at http://originalfalcon.com